Redefining Post–Traditional Learning:

Emerging Research and Opportunities

Lorie Cook–Benjamin
Doane University, USA

Jared Cook
Doane University, USA

A volume in the Advances in
Higher Education and Professional
Development (AHEPD) Book Series

T0408465

Published in the United States of America by
    IGI Global
    Information Science Reference (an imprint of IGI Global)
    701 E. Chocolate Avenue
    Hershey PA, USA 17033
    Tel: 717-533-8845
    Fax: 717-533-8661
    E-mail: cust@igi-global.com
    Web site: http://www.igi-global.com

Copyright © 2020 by IGI Global. All rights reserved. No part of this publication may be reproduced, stored or distributed in any form or by any means, electronic or mechanical, including photocopying, without written permission from the publisher.
Product or company names used in this set are for identification purposes only. Inclusion of the names of the products or companies does not indicate a claim of ownership by IGI Global of the trademark or registered trademark.

Library of Congress Cataloging-in-Publication Data

Names: Cook-Benjamin, Lorie, 1962- author. | Cook, Jared, 1987- author.
Title: Redefining post-traditional learning : emerging research and
  opportunities / by Lorie Cook-Benjamin and Jared Cook.
Description: Hershey, PA : Information Science Reference, 2020. | Includes
  bibliographical references. | Summary: ""This book explores changing
  student demographics and offers recommendations to current teaching
  methodologies through the lens of andragogy"--Provided by publisher"--
  Provided by publisher.
Identifiers: LCCN 2019017995 | ISBN 9781799801498 (paperback) | ISBN
  9781799801450 (hardcover) | ISBN 9781799801467 (ebook)
Subjects: LCSH: Adult learning. | Adult education--Methodology.
Classification: LCC LC5225.L42 C668 2020 | DDC 374--dc23
LC record available at https://lccn.loc.gov/2019017995

This book is published in the IGI Global book series Advances in Higher Education and Professional Development (AHEPD) (ISSN: 2327-6983; eISSN: 2327-6991)

British Cataloguing in Publication Data
A Cataloguing in Publication record for this book is available from the British Library.

All work contributed to this book is new, previously-unpublished material.
The views expressed in this book are those of the authors, but not necessarily of the publisher.

For electronic access to this publication, please contact: eresources@igi-global.com.

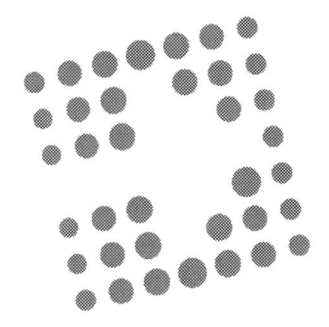

Advances in Higher Education and Professional Development (AHEPD) Book Series

ISSN:2327-6983
EISSN:2327-6991

Editor-in-Chief: Jared Keengwe, University of North Dakota, USA

MISSION

As world economies continue to shift and change in response to global financial situations, job markets have begun to demand a more highly-skilled workforce. In many industries a college degree is the minimum requirement and further educational development is expected to advance. With these current trends in mind, the **Advances in Higher Education & Professional Development (AHEPD) Book Series** provides an outlet for researchers and academics to publish their research in these areas and to distribute these works to practitioners and other researchers.

AHEPD encompasses all research dealing with higher education pedagogy, development, and curriculum design, as well as all areas of professional development, regardless of focus.

COVERAGE

- Adult Education
- Assessment in Higher Education
- Career Training
- Coaching and Mentoring
- Continuing Professional Development
- Governance in Higher Education
- Higher Education Policy
- Pedagogy of Teaching Higher Education
- Vocational Education

IGI Global is currently accepting manuscripts for publication within this series. To submit a proposal for a volume in this series, please contact our Acquisition Editors at Acquisitions@igi-global.com or visit: http://www.igi-global.com/publish/.

The Advances in Higher Education and Professional Development (AHEPD) Book Series (ISSN 2327-6983) is published by IGI Global, 701 E. Chocolate Avenue, Hershey, PA 17033-1240, USA, www.igi-global.com. This series is composed of titles available for purchase individually; each title is edited to be contextually exclusive from any other title within the series. For pricing and ordering information please visit http://www.igi-global.com/book-series/advances-higher-education-professional-development/73681. Postmaster: Send all address changes to above address. ©© 2020 IGI Global. All rights, including translation in other languages reserved by the publisher. No part of this series may be reproduced or used in any form or by any means – graphics, electronic, or mechanical, including photocopying, recording, taping, or information and retrieval systems – without written permission from the publisher, except for non commercial, educational use, including classroom teaching purposes. The views expressed in this series are those of the authors, but not necessarily of IGI Global.

Titles in this Series

For a list of additional titles in this series, please visit:
https://www.igi-global.com/book-series/advances-higher-education-professional-develop-
ment/73681

Workforce Education at Oil and Gas Companies in the Permian Basin Emerging Research and Opportunities
Julie Neal (Dearing Sales, USA) and Brittany Lee Neal (Axip Energy Services, USA)
Business Science Reference • ©2019 • 131pp • H/C (ISBN: 9781522584643) • US $160.00

Handbook of Research on Educator Preparation and Professional Learning
Drew Polly (University of North Carolina at Charlotte, USA) Christie Martin (University of South Carolina at Columbia, USA) and Kenan Dikilitaş (Bahçeşehir University, Turkey)
Information Science Reference • ©2019 • 459pp • H/C (ISBN: 9781522585831) • US $245.00

Preparing the Higher Education Space for Gen Z
Heidi Lee Schnackenberg (State University of New York at Plattsburgh, USA) and Christine Johnson (University of Western Kentucky, USA)
Information Science Reference • ©2019 • 253pp • H/C (ISBN: 9781522577638) • US $175.00

Competency-Based and Social-Situational Approaches for Facilitating Learning in Higher Education
Gabriele I.E. Strohschen (DePaul University, USA) and Kim Lewis (DePaul University, USA)
Information Science Reference • ©2019 • 317pp • H/C (ISBN: 9781522584889) • US $185.00

Autoethnography and Heuristic Inquiry for Doctoral-Level Researchers Emerging Research and Opportunities
Robin Throne (Northcentral University, USA)
Information Science Reference • ©2019 • 163pp • H/C (ISBN: 9781522593652) • US $135.00

Global Perspectives on Fostering Problem-Based Learning in Chinese Universities
Zhiliang Zhu (Northeastern University, China) and Chunfang Zhou (Aalborg University, Denmark)
Information Science Reference • ©2019 • 350pp • H/C (ISBN: 9781522599616) • US $195.00

For an entire list of titles in this series, please visit:
https://www.igi-global.com/book-series/advances-higher-education-professional-develop-
ment/73681

701 East Chocolate Avenue, Hershey, PA 17033, USA
Tel: 717-533-8845 x100 • Fax: 717-533-8661
E-Mail: cust@igi-global.com • www.igi-global.com

Table of Contents

Foreword

Changing landscape of higher education, traditional demographics drastically changing, and increasing need to have flexible options for learners are phrases heard across the country as we talk about the future of higher education. More than sixty percent of students enrolled are now over twenty-five and more than sixty percent of students are now working full-time while pursuing their education. Post-traditional students are quickly becoming the majority of the higher education student population.

My passion for supporting how post-traditional students learn best developed from understanding how I spent most of early career and education focused on the traditional student development and programming; yet the populations I began working with were not traditional. Therefore, I have spent most of my 17-year higher education career has been devoted to studying and learning more about post-traditional learners. When I began my doctoral degree, Adult and Higher Education, I began to understand how I could shift how I provide experiences to this increasing post-traditional student population.

One of my first courses in my doctoral program focused on how post-traditional students may have more, and different, concerns than a traditional student. Post-traditional students are preoccupied with these life concerns (food, sleep, bills, children, serving in military, and other concerns) learning becomes increasing more challenging (Merriam, Caffarella, & Baumgartner, 2007). Higher education faculty and staff can provide post-traditional students assistance by understanding that they bring a unique perspective to learning. Merriam, Caffarella, and Baumgartner (2007) discuss how important it is to understand that adult learners bring the following to the classroom and to co-curricular programming:

- Learners bring life experience and knowledge;
- Learners are goal oriented;
- Leaners need learning to be relevant to work;

- Learners need to be self-directing
- Learners approach learning through life situations and tend to be task-centered

Post-traditional students are a wealth of information and have purpose in learning. Those who work with post-traditional students can help them feel part of the learning experience by engaging them in the classroom, learning from their experiences, helping them define goals, tie learning to their work, and provide a variety of learning environments.

The authors of this book are clearly passionate about helping post-traditional students learn. The authors will inspire you to want to reimagine the educational experience for our increasing post-traditional student population.

Keegan Nichols
Arkansas Tech University, USA

Keegan Nichols, a native of Arkansas, was named Vice President for Student Affairs at Arkansas Tech University in June 2017. She currently serves on the board of the Arkansas Student Affairs Association, as a Higher Learning Commission Peer Reviewer, National Panhellenic Area Advisor, and NASPA Region IV-W Professional Standards Chair. Dr. Nichols has co-authored numerous articles and is committed to student success.

REFERENCES

Merriam, S. B., Caffarella, R. S., & Baumgartner, L. M. (2007). *Jossey-bass higher and adult education series. Learning in adulthood: A comprehensive guide* (3rd ed.). Hoboken, NJ: John Wiley & Sons Inc.

Preface

Higher education is changing. With each year, the need for technical and advanced degrees increases. Considering these vast changes, this book seeks to explore how higher education can better understand returning learners, specifically, the post-traditional learner population.

Chapter 1 overviews the purpose of this book. In the introductory chapter, the authors seek to define the term post-traditional learner, as well as the interdisciplinary research approach the authors utilize, and share the rationale for the book.

Chapter 2 explores traditional theorists as they apply to our current context in higher education. With a more diverse learner population entering higher education institutions, administrators and instructors need to recognize and utilize the building blocks of the theory that have brought higher education to where it is today. Included is not only traditional theorists, but their back, major concepts of the theory, how the theory applies to current administrators and instructors, and reference materials to learn more. Finally, case studies are included that provide opportunities to synthesize chapter information and provide discussion.

Chapter 3 outlines several learning approaches. Each learning approach has a base summary followed by the context that the approach can be utilized when working with post-traditional learners. After the initial summaries and takeaways, the authors delve into a learning approach framework they have designed surrounding social constructivism.

In Chapter 4, the authors consider Pedagogy to Andragogy. Readers are treated to a brief overview of the pedagogical history, and fine out when the change from pedagogy to andragogy occurred. Readers will also realize the definition of pedagogy and that pedagogical approaches can be placed on a spectrum from teacher-centered or teacher-directed to learner-centered or learner-directed. The term engagement and, more specifically, student engagement are presented in the chapter. Banking theory will be explored as well as false generosity, active learning, faculty development and the Community of Inquiry Framework.

In Chapter 5, the authors focus on administrators as a significant influence on a post-traditional learner's experience in higher education. As administrators, you have a unique role in the support of post-traditional learners.

In Chapter 6, the authors present the major takeaways for instructors. As with administrators, instructors have a unique role in teaching and serving post-traditional learners. The chapter includes case studies to better understand how to engage learners.

Chapter 7 represents concluding thoughts as well as a recap of some of the overarching critical recommendations from the book. This chapter includes takeaways from the theories presented, as well as takeaways from the instructor and administrator chapters. Finally, the authors wrap up the chapter and book with comments on research ideas for administrators and instructors. These research ideas represent potential ways for both administrators and instructors to help engage the post-traditional learner population and support further research.

Chapter 8 contains supplemental case studies for readers to consider from either the administrator or instructor point of view. While there are some that are written specifically for administrators or instructors, the majority of the case studies allow you to view the scenario from either lens. At the end of each case are several questions to provoke reflection and thought on the case study.

Acknowledgment

First, I'd like to thank my wife, who is standing directly behind me as I type this. Surely that did NOT influence me thanking her first. But seriously, Edith has been the emotional bedrock that's kept me going and grounded throughout this entire process. Without her, this book would not have happened.

Second, to my co-author, Lorie. It has been an amazing experience learning from you through this process, and I have become a well-rounded professional through this. Also, I want to thank all my friends and family who have given me support along the way. When I felt stressed throughout this process, not once did I feel a shred of doubt from those around me. It was this unwavering support from everyone in my life that helped me get here.

-Jared Cook

To the many learners and colleagues that I've encountered throughout my professional career, thank you, for helping me learn from and to grow with you. To my co-author, Jared, I'm inspired by your immense desire to learn and willingness to navigate with me as we figured out how to write this book, together. We did it! I'm grateful to be a part of your life and so proud of what you've already accomplished. Finally, to my husband, Don, you've been my constant supporter, promoter and believed in me even when I didn't believe in myself.

-Lorie Cook-Benjamin

Chapter 1
The Real Question:
Why Write This Book?

ABSTRACT

This chapter overviews the purpose of this book and is designed to help the readers leave a legacy, but only by adapting, changing, and designing policies, procedures, and classroom experiences that serve our students will that legacy come to fruition. Institutions with strong visions, missions, and legacies create traditions but also leave room for flexibility to work in this dynamic and changing global environment. In the introductory chapter, the authors seek to define the term post-traditional learner, as well as the interdisciplinary research approach the authors utilize, and share the rationale for the book.

JARED COOK'S MEMORIES

One of my most vivid educational moments came from my master's program several years ago, and, arguably, became the catalyst for my desire to write this book. Several years ago, a guest lecturer was invited to class. Here is a summary of his story.

Picture a young man growing up several decades ago. Times were good. He was younger, a full-time student, and could dedicate most of his time to studies. For work, he spent the summer working full-time in the fields, came back with enough money to pay for tuition, and some pocket change on the side for the rest of the year.

DOI: 10.4018/978-1-7998-0145-0.ch001

Copyright © 2020, IGI Global. Copying or distributing in print or electronic forms without written permission of IGI Global is prohibited.

Fast forward to the year 1995; he's been a university president for eight years. The enrollment is soaring, he's making changes and helping his university thrive. Fast forward again to 2015; he's retiring after 28 years of being president. Enrollment has grown at the institution for the past 17 years. International partnerships with several countries have led to increased revenue. Now, this is a true story, but here is what struck me. It wasn't his service, nor the institution's high enrollment, or that a third of the total budget came from international ventures, nor was it his dedication to the same university for 28 years. It was the fact that he could dedicate himself to a single venture, work, or education, all while having enough money to support himself.

At the heart of our institutions is our students. Without understanding his students, the 28-year legacy wouldn't have existed. This book is designed to help you leave a legacy, but only by adapting, changing, and designing policies, procedures, and classroom experiences that serve our students will that legacy come into fruition. Institutions with strong visions, missions, and legacies create traditions but also leave room for flexibility to work in this dynamic and changing global environment.

Presently, there are a few challenges to the focused approach of the past. Public state tuition has increased by over 237% on average in the past 20 years (Boyington, 2017). Paying tuition from a summer's salary is, for most people, long gone. With rising financial costs, as well as decreases in state funding, students are forced to adapt to this new realization. State funding has decreased by nearly nine billion dollars over the past ten years, leading to many institutions cutting corners and passing the buck to students (Mitchell, Leachman, & Masterson, 2017).

So where does this leave us? As administrators, instructors, and potentially students ourselves, we need to adjust. Quickly, efficiently, and intentionally, without sacrificing the cornerstone of our institutions' quality education. With rising costs and students' needs, it is no longer viable to rely solely on the original works by Mezirow (2000), Tinto (1981), Knowles (1980) or Tough (1971). Instead, we must place into service these base theorists to move a new set of guidelines forward, guidelines that emphasize the growing changes in our society due to changing economics and disruptive technology. By embracing these changes, you and we, will stand to gain a better understanding of your and our students. You and we, will also find ways to approach issues with policies and procedures that could affect student stop-out rates.

In this introduction, we seek to define the term post-traditional learner. You will be introduced to the interdisciplinary research approach utilized in the book as well as the rationale for why we, your authors, choses to write this book.

DEFINING TRADITIONAL AND POST-TRADITIONAL LEARNERS

Traditionally, traditional learners have been the emphasis of higher education... traditionally (Did we say that enough times?) With the explosion of access from newer and, at times, lower cost technology like cellular phones, higher education has seen an increase in the number of learners with what used to be called non-traditional, but now called post-traditional learners.

To contrast this significant change, let's compare the definitions of traditional learners, non-traditional learners, and post-traditional learners. For consistency in our definitions, we will use the National Center for Education Statistics' (NCES, 2017) explanation of each.

Traditional

The easiest of the three terms, traditional learners come directly out of high school. The National Center for Education Statistics (NCES, 2017) defines this group as "...enrolling immediately after high school and attending full time" (p. 1). Traditional learners are the group we traditionally (See what we did here?) support, that consumes our student support services, while leaving our other learners with less supported programs or services (You're starting to see a pattern here, we're sure).

Fact check: How many learners are some form of non-traditional?
30%? 50%? Try 85%.
In 2013, close to 85% of undergraduate students are considered some form of non-traditional (Soares, 2013, p. 6). For all our highlighters: Over 85% of all postsecondary learners are now some form of non-traditional. That means all those traditions, policies, and procedures that have existed for years and years, account for 15% of our current learners. In short, the learning landscape has changed, and higher education needs to re-adjust itself, fast. We're pleased to share there is good news as several researchers are challenging traditional practices and policies. Soares (2013) is credited with providing the first real update in several years to the concept of non-traditional learners.

Non-Traditional

Written in the retention realm, non-traditional learners find themselves labeled by the risk or attrition factors associated with their statistics.

"...The criteria chosen to identify nontraditional learners pertain to choices and behavior that may increase learners' risk of attrition and as such, are amenable to change or intervention at various stages in a learner's school life. With this intention, three sets of criteria were used to identify nontraditional learners: 1) enrollment patterns, 2) financial and family statistics, and 3) high school graduation statistics." (National Center for Education Statistics, 2017)

As you can see, non-traditional learners are seen less as a learner and more by the factors associated with how they arrive or why they leave a higher education institution. Imagine if learners found out that the label consistently used for them may be about their reasons for dropping out.

Post-Traditional Learner

Upon realizing that labeling learners due to their risk factors was not the best idea (Who knew?), scholars started to identify different ways to not only change the way to define learners but how to define them. Soares (2013), made what we would argue is the single most significant change to this idea of identifying learners. Soares defined post-traditional learners as those who are 25 or older, and are "individuals already in the workforce who lack a postsecondary credential yet are determined to pursue further knowledge and skills while balancing work, life, and education responsibilities" (p. 1). For those following along, you can easily tell the difference between these the last two concepts. But what specific types of students fall under this new definition, that is, post-traditional learners?

Fun fact: Vincent Tinto, author of one of the seminal works on retention, has written several articles and essays calling for a shift from retention toward persistence! You can read his essay on change at: Tinto, V. (2016, September, 26). From retention to persistence. *Inside Higher Ed*. Retrieved from https://www.insidehighered.com/views/2016/09/26/how-improve-student-persistence-and-completion-essay

THE FIVE COMMONALITIES OF POST-TRADITIONAL LEARNERS

Post-traditional learners differ from their traditional and non-traditional counterparts not only in definition, but also, in the outside roles that contribute to them being an adult learner. The five common factors of post-traditional learners include the following:

1. *Are needed wage earners for themselves or their families;*
2. *Combine work and learning at the same time or move between them frequently;*
3. *Pursue knowledge, skills, and credentials that employers will recognize and compensate;*
4. *Require developmental education to be successful in college-level courses; and*
5. *Seek academic/career advising to navigate their complex path to a degree*
   (Soares, 2013, p. 2).

Understanding the Post-Traditional Student Population

Students, who are in some form non-traditional, compose an impressive 85% of the undergraduate population. Here's the breakdown of these students as outlined by Soares (2013).

Factor #1 - Undergraduate Age

"38 percent of those enrolled are over the age of 25 and one-fourth are over the age of 30" (Soares, 2013, p. 6). Considering this statistic, the percentage of undergraduate students entering college later in life is continuously increasing, with students over 25 set to increase another 23% by the end of 2019 (Soares, 2013).

Factor #2 - Federal Grants

Changes to undergraduate populations lead to changes in federal funding, with the average age of a Pell Grant recipient currently at 26 (Soares, 2013). Changes to federal funding, including legislative changes protecting student rights, with the average age continuing to rise over the last 20 years (Soares, 2013).

Factor #3 - Undergraduate Families

Families are a defining role for many students. While years ago they may have disqualified students from attending college, this is no longer the case. "Nearly a quarter of postsecondary students in the United States (3.9 million) are parents. Half of the student parents are married, and half are unmarried" (Soares, 2013, p. 6). Student-parents split between those married and unmarried is a statistic that deserves special attention. Students who are unmarried, taking care of one or more children may have less outside support in college, but have no less desire to complete their degree. As the momentum increases for this factor, this will be a crucial group for administrators and instructors to consider.

Factor #4 - University Breakdown

Depending on which type of university system you are in, the breakdown of your student demographics can heavily influence policy. Soares, (2013), states "43 percent of all undergraduates attend community colleges. And, adult learners make up as much as 60 percent of all community college students" (p. 6). For community college administrators, post-traditional students should be a major area of focus for your campus. Four-year regional colleges fear not, your statistic is also laudable. "30 percent of undergraduates enrolled at public four-year regional colleges and universities are adults over the age of 24" (Soares, 2013, p. 6). With almost a third of students in the post-traditional territory, this is a great time to reconsider your policies and procedures to serve post-traditional student needs.

Factor #5 - Part-Timers

"Almost 40 percent of all undergraduates and about 60 percent of those attending public two-year colleges are enrolled part-time" (Soares, 2013, p. 6). While this statistic *should* be evident in our policies and procedures, consider what many institutions view for retention goals. Universities heavily tout four and five-year completion statistics with policies that support these notions of completion, yet, if you look at a post-traditional student looking to complete their undergraduate degree going part-time (120 credit hours, 6 per semester), that student could take anywhere from 5 - 10 years to complete those twenty semesters. Does a person who takes ten years to complete their undergraduate degree constitute a success or a failure? With these ideas in mind, we will continue to explore the world of post-traditional learners.

Why the Change: Non-Traditional to Post-Traditional Learners

Why the change? What prompted the need to create a new definition? The answer is both simple and complex.

The incredibly complex version in three words? Technology, budgets, and globalization. Disruptive technology has completely changed who has access to education, making longstanding student definitions have little to no meaning. Globalization has also become a disruptor to higher education, with a change from the local and national level to global education. Described in a later section of this chapter, budgets have also changed the landscape.

Refresher area:
● Traditional = High school learners who enroll full time at an institution after graduating.
● Non-traditional = Risk/attrition factors of learner.
● Post-traditional = Determined individuals seeking knowledge and work/life balance.

The simple version. Higher education institutions could no longer hide from the elephant in the room. That elephant was the pressure of outside politicians and employers calling for increased accountability, in addition to a changing population that needed different styles of education to address their needs better. The Association of American Colleges & Universities (2015), conducted a survey looking at employer needs, finding that "Nearly all employers surveyed (91 percent) say that a demonstrated capacity to think critically, communicate clearly, and solve complex problems is more important than [a candidate's] undergraduate major" (p. 1). This shift included undergraduate majors, with 58% of employers saying: "improvements are needed to prepare students for success in entry-level positions" (Association of American Colleges & Universities, 2015, p. 1).

Disruptive Technology and Post-Traditional Learner Needs

Do you remember near the year 2000 and the craze over the end of the digital world because of the Y2K bug? Somehow, thankfully, we are still here, and so is our digital world. Technology has become the center of conversation in higher education, and there is no shortage of reasons. Consider the following, as of 2016, roughly 88% of adults use the internet (Pew Research Center, 2017). In context, only 52% of adults used the internet in 2000 (Pew Research Center, 2017). Imagine that only about half of adults used the internet near the Y2K craze! A statistic from two years ago indicated that eight out of ten adults now use the internet.

With changes in technology, the global market, and overall access to education, a shift has occurred in society's expectations of higher education. New expectations include global awareness, along with a sense of immediacy for higher education. Our learners can no longer afford to be only regionally engaged, and institutions that understand this have already started moving forward. Disruptive technology (e.g., the internet) has allowed progressive universities to take the stage, designing Massive Open Online Courses (MOOC's) and developing online programs that engage post-traditional learners in a way traditional higher education has yet to accomplish.

While access to new technology has been a boon for a large number of learners and universities, American higher education institutions still face challenges in the way they engage their online and international learners. Between 2004 to 2014, the number of learners aged 25 or older increased by 18%, leading to an increase in many online post-traditional learners (National Center for Education Statistics, 2016). Many online formats rely on slide presentations, videos, or writing prompts. These, not so engaging activities, leave learners facing a challenge when they step into the online classroom. Between passive lectures that border on using Banking theory to a lack of classroom interaction that Tinto (2017) describes as a necessary component for persistence, many post-traditional learners find themselves with access to a university, but a lackluster alternative to the physical classroom. Disruptive

---

Consider your current university. Have there been any changes in policy that allows learners to participate in MOOC's and receive credit? Are there ways aside from dual credit for learners to transfer in the wealth of knowledge they have from previous work experiences? How does your current curriculum show that you acknowledge learner's experiences outside the classroom?

---

technology has become a dominant driving force within higher education and will continue to change the way we work with post-traditional learners online. Higher education is noted for changing at a glacial pace. While new policies, procedures, and techniques are introduced, higher education has maintained vigilance in its attempt to keep long-held traditions, including a longstanding agrarian cycle of teaching, passive lecture styles that seem eerily similar to Banking theory, and a curriculum designed for learners following a linear life path. Through this book, we seek to address the crumbling infrastructure of higher education, inform potential instructors and administrators of the challenges and opportunities formed by disruptive technology and learner demographics, and finally provide options to better assist learners in policy, practice, and persistence, both inside and outside the classroom.

Globalization and Higher Education

Globalization has also become a driving force for higher education. Qiang (2003), notes "The recruitment of foreign learners has become a significant factor for institutional income and of national economic interest" (p. 249). For post-traditional learners, the needs of a globally focused education continue to increase. While America has seen an increase in the national agenda to educate more of the population, "private actors" operating in the education world has led to a blurring of national borders (Qiang, 2003, p. 249). The blurring of national borders and the increase of private actors (e.g., businesses, philanthropists) has led to the need for higher education institutions to better educate their post-traditional learner populations on global matters. The climate of and the job market, for those returning to the education world, has changed. Center to the conversation is an article written by Lanford and Maruco (2018), which highlights the current struggle in America between liberal or professional (vocational) education. While an emphasis on a broad, liberal curriculum is a way to engage learner critical thinking and soft skills, this runs contrary to the competing demands of the job market, which proponents of professional education believe that an emphasis on a specific vocational area will better assist learners facing socio-economic barriers in their journey to success (Lanford & Maruco, 2018). This debate is a microcosm of the higher education debate worldwide, which Qiang (2003) notes "…that higher education has now become a real part of the globalization process: the cross-

> While certifications have been around for years, the influx of accessibility from technology has caused certifications to take the world by storm and not just in the business world. One of the biggest gripes regarding higher education is the longstanding foundation surrounding degree credit hours. Traditionally, institutions will offer associates, bachelors, masters, and, on rare occasions, a single type of certification. While there have been certifications around for a long time, progressive institutions are picking up on the trend for post-bachelor's certificates. Instead of offering a full bachelors or masters, some certifications grant you access to specific therapies, counseling, business approaches, etc. Progressive institutions are seeing the value in shortening credit hours, and instead focusing on providing particular skill sets to learners. [One could even say providing post-traditional learners with a 'very particular set of skills.' Oh, the terrible jokes will keep coming.] The success of this approach which we'll cover later in the theory chapter, is that learners feel a sense of self-efficacy and may continue on their path towards completion. Learners also understand the value of the curriculum, as it may help avoid classes they don't view as valuable, although research shows liberal arts curriculums hold an intrinsic value.

border matching of supply and demand" (p. 249). With supply and demand of post-traditional learners taking center stage in the job market, a curriculum that emphasizes a global context will continue to permeate higher education in the coming years, and, thus, becomes an essential part of the system.

Budgets and the Bloated Classroom

As institutions proceed through the 21st century, the proliferation of technology has created a new era enabling post-traditional learners to enter universities despite geographical barriers. Using census data, the percentage of post-traditional learners has increased dramatically. From 1970 to 2017, the total number of learners with some degree of non-traditional-ness (i.e., part-time job, part-time learner) has reached roughly 85% (National Center for Education Statistics, 2017). The last census showed "4 out of 10 undergraduate learners are over 24 and enrolled on a part-time basis" (Wyatt, 2011, p. 1). This increase in learner diversity means a much larger base of learners with real-life experience rarely seen before at the undergraduate level and is a significant population that the majority of higher education institutions have yet to accommodate intentionally. Hake (1999) referred to this concept as "detraditionalization" (p. 4), in which learners are less influenced by traditions and more influenced by globalization. Even though post-traditional learners have been studied heavily by universities in areas such as improving recruiting techniques or online learning, research is lacking on effective teaching strategies for this type of learner in undergraduate classrooms.

At the undergraduate level and in face to face settings, post-traditional learners find themselves in bloated classrooms with little access to resources that fit their needs. Consider general education required courses. These courses could be pre-requisite classes for majors or classes that learners are required to take. Many universities have targeted pre-requisite classes to help mitigate costs, partially due to decreases in state funding. Remember, state funding has decreased by nearly nine billion dollars over the past ten years, leading to institutions cutting corners to continue to exist (Mitchell, Leachman & Masterson, 2017). In addition to cutting corners, average tuition has increased. In-state tuition at a public university has risen by 237% on average in the past 20 years (Boyington, 2017). With all of these factors affecting higher education, many required courses are becoming the focal point of institution savings. Each discipline hosts similar classes and usually have some common characteristics, for example,

a larger than average class size for the university. Since so many learners are required to take the course, this becomes a cost-cutting area for universities. This large class may find a professor using transmittal techniques, such as lecture, presentation slides or video as their primary teaching tool due to the large class sizes and the ease of use of such methods. Additionally, standard testing assessments focusing on quizzes, tests, or other easy to grade assignments, may be found because these assessments require less work and time for the professor.

While these techniques may benefit the professors through reduced workload and the university due to the increased number of learners in a class section, post-traditional undergraduate learners are suffering in these classes. Torres (1994) explained that most college professors "do not address objective reality" (p. 23). Instead, professors focus on a book and journal objective reality, which not only devalues learner experiences but also lacks the real-world context in which learners will work or are working. Part of the issue in many of these classes rests with a lack of resources, which includes outsourcing many courses to adjuncts. By 2011, 70% of faculty were considered contingent, which consists of all faculty who did not qualify for the tenure track (Edmonds, 2015). Often, both adjunct faculty and many contingent faculty are provided less professional development than tenured faculty, creating a gap in teaching methods between the faulty considered contingent and tenured or tenured track faculty.

In addition to the classes lacking real-world context, Monks and Schmidt (2011) explain in their analysis of class size and students on outcomes that "the evidence found in this analysis unequivocally leads to the conclusion that class size has a negative impact on the learner-rated outcomes of amount learned, instructor rating, and course rating" (p. 15). These large class sizes continue to be a mainstay in many institutions, despite well-documented issues. In this changing time, higher education needs to understand "the one-size-fits-all lecture hall is becoming obsolete" (Burke-Vigeland et al., 2011, p. 1).

The ideas of adult learning and the needs of post-traditional learners have been around since the early 20th century. While Dewey is credited with much of the American ideals on adult learning, Eduard Lindeman's 1926 *The Meaning of Adult Education* provides a broad context pertinent to the discussion of post-traditional learners. As far back as the early 20th century, a struggle existed between the attempts of nations to standardize learning and the needs of individual learners. Lindeman (1926) writes about efforts to allow free access to education and to standardize education, saying:

We have gone even further and have made certain levels of education compulsory. But the result has been disappointing; we have succeeded merely in formalizing, mechanizing educational processes. The spirit and meaning of education cannot be enhanced by addition, by the easy method of giving the same dose to more individuals. (p. 4)

As we consider the current climate in higher education institutions, the main issue facing post-traditional learners is the idea of standardization. Generally, liberal arts institutions require students to complete a set curriculum. Patricia Cross (1992), touches on this concept, looking at how mandatory education in adult education is turning attempts to learn into a duty, rather than a self-pursued interest. While some higher education institutions argue a liberal education provides a well-rounded individual, when analyzing post-traditional learners' needs, there are stark differences in the needs of each learner, and the standardized curriculums may not offer the skills needed by employers.

A study by the Association of American Colleges & Universities (2015) found that "nearly all employers surveyed (91 percent) say that a demonstrated capacity to think critically, communicate clearly, and solve complex problems is more important than [a candidate's] undergraduate major" (p. 1). Employers' needs should be carefully balanced with learners needing a liberal arts education. Furthermore, in the same 2015 study, 58% of employers said: "improvements are needed to prepare learners for success in entry-level positions" (Association of American Colleges & Universities, 2015, p. 1). This need for improvement places pressures on higher education institutions to evolve and better serve learners. We argue the best place to begin is at the undergraduate level.

Standardization permeates, not only institutions' curricula but professor's curricula as well. As far back as the 1920s, Lindeman (1926) pointed out this issue, writing: "In conventional education, the learner is required to adjust himself to an established curriculum; in adult education, the curriculum is built around the learner's needs and interests" (p. 6). This seemingly backward approach to education is one of the primary reasons post-traditional learners may view colleges as foreign, complex places, especially in the context of undergraduate classes designed for traditional learners. Lindeman (1926) attempts to explain this difference and uses the idea of imagination versus experience to help demonstrate pedagogical and andragogical differences, seeking to highlight that adult learning makes use of learners' experiences versus providing learners imagined examples of issues.

Harris (1980) in his book, *Comparative Adult Education*, echoes Lindeman's sentiment on curriculum, focusing more on the mentality of administrators at the university, state, and national level. When considering formal education systems, Harris writes "their [administrators] main focus is always on stability rather than reform" (p. 10). This focus on stability has allowed higher education institutions to persist but has slowed change. The lack of willingness for reform or change is an issue both Lindeman and Harris believe persists, with Harris (1980) stating "while adult education, too, is in part involved in a similar equipping of adult, it is equally and deeply involved also in every aspect (political, social, 'spiritual', and material) of adult society itself" (p. 10).

Chapter One Summary: From Complex Questions to Simple Solutions

We've thrown a lot of facts, both new and old at you, so what does this mean? In short, higher education is dealing with a problem that's been around since the 1920s and even earlier across the globe. Higher education has consistently stayed its ground, although, slowly, external pressure is now forcing higher education to reconsider its traditional delivery system. The days of only the traditional learner are gone. Today, only 15% of our current population still follow the traditional linear path that, for decades, has been the sustenance of higher education. Globalization, technology, and budgets have caused us to reconsider how we engage learners. Progressive institutions are already embracing learners in various ways. These ways include reducing credit hours, offering certifications, night classes, blended or online courses, and emphasizing globally engaged learners. For the rest of us, if we don't change soon, learners will become dissatisfied with our institutions and choose others more accommodating, leaving enrollment numbers at an all-time low, with less and less money to invest in new initiatives.

To navigate these complexities, we need to understand and engage our post-traditional learner populations. Understanding their unique needs, not only benefits post-traditional learners but supports other learners.

For instructors, understanding what learners need in the classroom and how to intentionally engage them, is an excellent first step, and will be examined in subsequent chapters. For administrators, supporting both your instructors, as well as designing and implementing policies that match the flexibility needed by post-traditional learners, is your first step. More on this topic will also be covered in subsequent chapters.

The following is a case study of an incoming post-traditional learner. Before we dive into theory (chapters 2 and 3), post-traditional needs (chapter 2), and how to support post-traditional learners (chapters 4-6), use your current knowledge to see how you would approach the following case study. Consider the chapter's material, and identify not only your current role but look at it from the perspective of your instructor or an administrative counterpart. Identify the services, support, and needs of the post-traditional learner.

Case Study: School, Children, Work. Repeat

Edith, a new undergraduate student, sits nervously in your office. Part of the new fall orientation requires new students meet with faculty and administrators to identify potential mentors and increase persistence. You start the conversation with a few open-ended questions given to you by an advisor-friend. Edith reveals that she has been out of school for several years, working different jobs before finally deciding to come and obtain her undergraduate degree. She's nervous about her ability to learn after being gone so long, and she's also balancing several other roles. Edith is a mother and a full-time worker. She shares that she's unsure of what she needs to do to be successful, staring at you intently. What do you do?

You decide to explain some of the time commitments, equating each credit hour to roughly 3 hours of studying. You explain to her, by taking nine credit hours, she should expect to study anywhere from 18-20 hours per week. You

---

Administrators: What type of resources can you provide? Are there resources your current institution has available? What policies can you leverage to better support this student?
Instructors: What teaching strategies do you use to accommodate full-time workers? Are your deadlines arbitrarily difficult?

---

can tell Edith is fairly nervous about this commitment. You assure her that you will support her in the process, and schedule monthly meetings with her to give her advice. You also refer her to the academic support center, personally walking her there and having her meet the director, so she can feel more comfortable about receiving help in her studies.

Edith continues to meet with you each month. In the conversations, she lets you know her fears about her child and class commitments. Her daughter is young, and the current daycare she uses is not always open and will close early. You let her know that professors at the institution are flexible and try to work with students who have other obligations; however, Edith should be pro-active in conversing with her instructors.

Halfway Through the Semester

As you pass the midterm point in the semester, you receive a call from Edith asking to meet with you immediately. You schedule an appointment with her the following day. Edith comes into your office, looking as if she has cried all night. She explains to you that her daughter was sick, and she was unable to go to class for the midterm. She had e-mailed the professor, Dr. No Budge, but was told there were no makeups, gave her a zero for the midterm, and seemed unwilling to work with her. As you explore the mechanics of the class, you find out that the class has three tests that make up the entirety of the grade. Losing out on this midterm would mean at best. Edith would receive a D in the class.

You decide to consult with the department chair regarding the issue. While you considered going to the professor directly, the lack of willingness to work with Edith indicates this may not be the most appropriate choice. As you sit down to coffee with Dr. Chair, you engage in some casual conversation, before diving into the issue. "I'll be honest. I have some concerns relayed to me from one of my mentees that I want to bring up regarding Dr. No Budge." You explain the situation, including your mentee's situation, and the lack of flexibility shown in the course. "In short, I felt this was something best

---

Questions to consider:
How would you approach this situation?
Do you contact the instructor on Edith's behalf?
Do you contact the department chair?
Are there policies or procedures that better support Edith so she can earn a passing grade?

---

discussed with you, as I'm unsure of our next steps." Dr. Chair has a very serious look on her face, and says "This is something I will address, thank you for bringing it to my attention." You finish talking to Dr. Chair about other matters, before parting ways. You inform Edith that the department was receptive to the situation, and it should be resolved soon.

Edith is overjoyed and, later, sends you an e-mail that she will be allowed to take the midterm. She thanks you for your help, and continues to meet with you over the next months, and the following semester.

REFERENCES

Association of American Colleges & Universities. (2015, January 20). *Employers judge recent graduates ill-prepared for today's workplace, endorse broad and project-based learning as best preparation for career opportunity and long-term success.* Retrieved from http://www.aacu.org/press/press-rele ases/2015employerlearnersurveys

Boyington, B. (2017, September 20). See 20 years of tuition growth at national universities. *U.S. News.* Retrieved from https://www.usnews.com/education/ best-colleges/paying-for-college/articles/2017-09-20/see-20-years-of-tuition-growth-at-national-universities

Burke-Vigeland, M., Broz, D., Thaler, M., Barber, C., Hickson, K., LoBello, T., ... Rydell, S. (2011). *The Dynamics of Place in Higher Education.* Retrieved from https://www.gensler.com/research-insight/gensler-research-institute/ the-dynamics-of-place-in-higher-education

Donaldson, J., & Graham, S. (1999). A model of college outcomes for adults. *Adult Education Quarterly, 50*(1), 24–40. doi:10.1177/074171369905000103

Edmonds, D. (2015, May 28). More Than Half of College Faculty Are Adjuncts: Should You Care? *Forbes.* Retrieved from https://www.forbes. com/sites/noodleeducation/2015/05/28/more-than-half-of-college-faculty-are-adjuncts-should-you-care/#6e791ca01600

Hake, B. (1999). Lifelong learning in late modernity: The challenges of society, organizations and individuals. *Adult Education Quarterly, 49*(2), 79–90. doi:10.1177/074171369904900201

Harris, W. J. (1980). *Comparative adult education; Practice, purpose and theory.* New York: Addison-Wesley Longman Limited.

Knowles. (1980). *The modern practice of adult education.* New York: Cambridge, The Adult Education Company.

Lanford, M., & Maruco, T. (2018). When Job Training Is Not Enough: The Cultivation of Social Capital in Career Academies. *American Educational Research Journal, 55*(3), 617–648. doi:10.3102/0002831217746107

Lindeman, E. (1926). *The meaning of adult education.* New York: New Republic, Inc.

Mezirow, J., & ... (2000). *Learning as transformation: Critical perspectives on a theory in progress.* San Francisco, CA: Jossey-Bass.

Mitchell, M., Leachman, M., & Masterson, K. (2017, August 23). A Lost Decade in Higher Education Funding. *Center on Budget and Policy Priorities.* Retrieved from https://www.cbpp.org/research/state-budget-and-tax/a-lost-decade-in-higher-education-funding

Monks, J., & Schmidt, R. (2011). The impact of class size on outcomes in higher education. *The B.E. Journal of Economic Analysis & Policy, 11*(1). doi:10.2202/1935-1682.2803

National Center for Education Statistics. (2017). *Definitions and Data.* Retrieved from https://nces.ed.gov/pubs/web/97578e.asp

Pew Research Center. (2017, July 10). Sharp Partisan Divisions in Views of National Institutions. *Pew Research Center.* Retrieved from http://www.people-press.org/2017/07/10/sharp-partisan-divisions-in-views-of-national-institutions//

Qiang, Z. (2003). Internationalization of higher education: Towards a conceptual framework. *Policy Futures in America, 1*(2), 248–270. doi:10.2304/pfie.2003.1.2.5

Soares, L. (2013). Post-traditional learners and the transformation of postsecondary education: A manifesto for college leaders. *American Council of Education.* Retrieved from http://www.acenet.edu/news-room/Documents/Post-Traditional-Learners.pdf

Torres, C. A. (1994). Introduction. In *M. Escobar, A. L. Fernandez, & G. Guevara-Niebla (Eds.), Paulo Freire on higher education: A dialogue at the National University of Mexico* (pp. 1–25). Albany, NY: State University of New York Press.

Tough, A. (1981). *Learning without a teacher: A study of tasks and assistance during adult self-teaching projects.* Toronto: Ontario Institute for Studies in Education.

Wyatt, L. G. (2011). Nontraditional learner engagement: Increasing adult learner success and retention. *Journal of Continuing Higher Education, 59*(1), 10–20. doi:10.1080/07377363.2011.544977

Chapter 2
Traditional Theorists and You

ABSTRACT

This chapter explores traditional theorists as they apply to our current context in higher education. With a more diverse learner population entering higher education institutions, administrators and instructors need to recognize and utilize the building blocks of the theory that have brought higher education to where it is today. Included are not only traditional theorists, but their back, major concepts of the theory, how the theory applies to current administrators and instructors, and reference materials to learn more. Finally, case studies are included that provide opportunities to synthesize chapter information and provide discussion.

DOI: 10.4018/978-1-7998-0145-0.ch002

Copyright © 2020, IGI Global. Copying or distributing in print or electronic forms without written permission of IGI Global is prohibited.

INTRODUCTION

As this book explores the latest available research, understanding the theories, which helped to form them, is essential. To explore all aspects of each theory would take hundreds of pages and is really outside the scope of this book. Therefore, instead of regurgitating the entirety of each theory, we offer highlights and a summarization of each theory's main points, while also providing references to these seminal works. In this chapter, for each theory, you will find

1. reference materials to consider,
2. an overview of the theory's evolution,
3. major concepts from the theory, and
4. how the theory applies to current administrators and instructors; look for our takeaways in the boxes.

MALCOLM KNOWLES - ANDRAGOGY

Background

Malcolm Knowles is widely credited as the person who brought the concept of Andragogy to North America. As a theorist, his work noted some of the first significant assumptions and differences among adult learners in education and is a staple in almost any adult education course. For our purposes, Knowles (1980) believed several different assumptions would help educators to understand how best to support adult learners, and, in our case, post-traditional learners. Each of these assumptions provides a wealth of information related to post-traditional learner's needs, and how learners aren't offered intentional experiences in the classroom. We'll take an in-depth look at each of these assumptions, and how they serve as the basis for newer theories.

Core Concepts

Malcolm Knowles posits several assumptions, including changes in self-concept, orientation to learning, the role of experience, readiness to learn, and motivation to learn. Each of the following is summarized below.

Changes in Self-Concept

Changes in self-concept see an adult learner as one who has become self-directed in their lives. Knowles (1980) explains that individuals become adults when they get to the point of directing their own lives. Unpacking this notion, Knowles focuses on this idea of self-direction. Whereas, a viewpoint of a child or younger learner is dependent on their caregivers, teachers, and parental figures, adults have the independence to identify their own needs and pursue them independently. Bye, Pushkar and Conway (2007), note that "strong intrinsic motivation may be necessary for nontraditional learners to persist and succeed in the university environment over the long term" (p. 143). The changes in the adult learners' perceptions of priorities become one of the most critical factors in adult learners returning and persisting to earn their degrees. However, this perception of priorities often comes in conflict with an instructor's desire for students' learning. Learners who find themselves in classes that disallow self-direction will find instructors who naturally fail to assist post-traditional learners on their pathway to success.

This concept of the learner goes further to the devaluing of the learner's concept of self-direction. Regarding independent, self-directing learners, Knowles states (1980), "thus, when he/she [the self-directed adult learner] finds him/herself in a situation in which he/she is not allowed to be self-directing, he/she experiences a tension between that situation and his/her self-concept" (p. 56). It is worth noting that those who see themselves as self-directing adults, which encompasses our post-traditional learners, experience tension when education processes force them into the same educational situation as a younger learner who has yet to develop these ideas of independence, self-directedness and take on the mantle of adulthood. This has been reinforced by Wang (2014), who adds that "in the United States to catch up with learners in other industrialized nations including newly emerged China and India, SDL [self-directed learning] must be promoted and implemented at all levels of education, not only within adult education" (p. XV).

Fun Fact: If you want to fail early in your teaching career, don't let your learners engage in activities that allow self-direction.

Takeaways

Administrators: Self-concept is a building block that good administrators acknowledge, and account for when developing policies. Learners are major stakeholders at your institution and, if their ability to pursue educational goals is interrupted, they will develop internal coalitions with faculty and professional staff. If policies are stifling, learners may decide not to persist, which directly affects the health of the institution.

For those teaching: The classroom, whether online, blended, face to face or some other method is one of the most potent factors in student satisfaction, persistence, and knowledge gain at higher education institutions. By allowing learners to decide their path, whether through flexibility in learning activities, or engaging in discourse regarding the syllabus, empowering your learners to be a part of the learning experience changes learner experiences and teaching practices for the better.

The Role of Experience

Experience plays a valuable role in all learners' lives. Knowles (1980) explains that as learners mature, they gain an increasing amount of experience that can be an asset to the classroom content. Their experiences help learners to develop a deeper understanding of concepts and supplement the provided material using their own experiences. As post-traditional learners, many of these learners come to college with rich and diverse backgrounds. As discussed in the introduction, the landscape of what a 'traditional learner' means has changed. Donaldson and Graham, (1999), reviewed current globalization and found that, "furthermore, due to their rich personal experiences, adults can link new knowledge to an existing complex schema that in many cases allows them to make direct connections between new knowledge and its use" (p. 25). Isn't this what we want for our students? The new, diverse, and often more experienced learners provide instructors with an opportunity to tap into a wealth of knowledge and experience in the classroom, which may be a crucial link to bridge the gap between traditional and post-traditional learners. Along with understanding the effect of self-concept, specific techniques can be used that will empower instructors and provide a more deliberate and supportive learning process. Knowles (1980) writes "accordingly, in the technology of andragogy there is decreasing emphasis on the transmittal techniques of traditional teaching and increasing emphasis on experiential techniques which tap the experience of the learners and involve them in analyzing their experience" (p. 56). When we consider current teaching strategies, there are many classrooms, especially larger class sections which rely more heavily on transmittal techniques rather than experiential to engage learners. However, it is clear that these techniques belie the importance of professors providing intentional ways to use prior experience, as opposed to the continuous use of techniques which force learners into passive states. Knowles (1980) supports this difference in techniques, noting that *to a child, experience is something that happens to him; to an adult, experience is who he is. So in any situation in which an adult's experience is being devalued or ignored, the adult perceives this as not just rejecting his experiences, but rejecting him as a person. (p. 56)*

Without a focus on a post-traditional learner's prior knowledge, any teaching strategy used by an instructor would discount and devalue the experience of a post-traditional learner. We would argue that the majority of instructors do not intend to devalue their students and, once aware this is how students' perceive their teaching, would happily change their teaching practices.

Readiness to Learn

Post-traditional learners' needs, motivations, and interests vary depending on their roles in life, and on their current circumstances. As one of the main assumptions from Knowles (1980), it's important to view his reasoning in the context of our post-traditional learner's needs. Knowles explains the difference between what learners 'ought' to do and what adults 'need' to do. This differentiation between the extrinsic and intrinsic motivation of traditional and post-traditional learners is one of the defining factors between these two groups. One of the challenges Knowles (1980) writes about is the timing of learning experiences and developmental tasks. With our emphasis on the curriculum in higher education, we may miss the critical moment when a learner requires immediate knowledge on a subject, solely because we have scheduled it as a topic taught later in the term. Again, consider the plight of post-traditional learners in current undergraduate society. Are the classes pertinent and relevant to the learners' current state in life? Tsai, Li, and Cheng (2016) looked at this concept of relevant knowledge, specifically

---

Takeaways

Administrators: Learners need venues to use their previous experience. Hiring well-informed instructors that utilize active learning techniques will go a long way towards student knowledge retention, satisfaction, and soft skill development.

For those teaching: Out of the four assumptions, the role of experience is probably the most important for those teaching post-traditional learners. The role of experience cannot be understated when developing your activities, assessments, and outcomes. Well-designed classes that incorporate opportunities for reflection and use of previous experience increase student satisfaction, as well as classroom success. For instructors coming from departments that may use more traditional methods, for example, methods emphasizing passive learning, Freeman et al. (2014) in their study of the STEM field, found that active learning increased average exam scores by 6%, while learners were 1.5 times more likely to fail in classrooms that utilized traditional lectures. While there are some limitations due to this study's experimental design, the gains noted are an important step towards finding methods that help learners succeed.

> **Takeaways**
>
> **Administrators:** With an eye on curriculum, students' readiness can be positively or negatively affected by lack of flexibility, as well as lack of practical experiences. Bear in mind that some post-traditional learners are returning to higher education institutions with some experience, but may still benefit from the ability to utilize classroom practices in the form of internships, co-ops, or other intentional work experiences.
>
> **For those teaching:** As someone who dictates the type of experiences learners will interact with in the classroom, you are on the frontlines to make changes and support your learners. One of the primary reasons for this historical approach to theory is to help create a better understanding of how much we know and how much we can support our students' growth. If, that is, we pay attention to previous theory and how it's been updated. This includes the assumption by Knowles (1980), emphasizing student experiences in the classroom, whether the classroom is blended, online, or a face to face format.

at STEM interest in adults. These researchers found that providing adults with resources that increased self-efficacy in science led to more interest in the topic, and more pursuit by adults. While current curriculums offer scaffolding, one of the major drawbacks to the scaffolded curriculum and other strategies is a lack of flexibility related to learners' needs. In many traditional learners' eyes, the transmittal techniques may be relevant due to their previous and perhaps recent K-12 experience, but that experience is far different for many post-traditional learners, who have been out of this similar experience for several years. Knowles (1980) explains this idea in the following statement:

It is my observation that a good deal of professional education is totally out of phase with the learners' readiness to learn. For example, a new medical learner needs to have direct experience with hospitals, patients, and practicing doctors before he is ready to learn facts about pathology, anatomy, biochemistry, and other content. (p. 57)

An out of phase curriculum is still a topic heavily researched. In 2015, the Association of American Colleges & Universities found that 58% of employers said "improvements are needed to prepare learners for success in entry-level positions" (p. 1) and 91% of employers believe that "thinking critically, communicating clearly, and being able to solve complex problems is more important than candidates undergraduate major" (Association of American Colleges & Universities, 2015, p. 1). The next assumption from Knowles' (1980) work is Orientation to Learning.

Orientation to Learning

One of the main differences in younger learners' education versus post-traditional learners is their orientation to learning. For younger learners, much of their education revolves around subject centered content. The premise for this is that there are certain areas a learner needs to know before adulthood. For post-traditional learners, learning has shifted from a subject-centered curriculum to one of problem-centered education. Often, there are experiences in post-traditional learners' lives that require more knowledge, and often a sense of immediacy in gaining that knowledge. Knowles (1980) explains orientation to learning as:

The child's time perspective toward learning is one of postponed application. For example, much of what I learned in grade school had little to do with my functioning better as a preadolescent; I learned it to be able to get into high school. (p. 58)

This focus on the postponed application is entirely different than a post-traditional learners' mindset. The sense of immediacy from experience means a post-traditional learner requires the knowledge for immediate use, rather than using it later. This change in mentality is a building block for quality, as it becomes one criterion for noting whether the curriculum is providing opportunities for immediate use of the content, instead of creating simple building blocks to be used later. When we consider undergraduate education, especially in institutions' requiring 100 level classes, the need for immediacy is often not granted, thus requiring our institutions to find other teaching strategies to better fulfill the needs of post-traditional learners.

Motivation to Learn

One of the most applicable assumptions that Knowles (1980) posits is that learners mature and their motivation becomes internal, rather than external. Extrinsic motivation is something you've probably seen before from childhood until now. It's the program "BOOK IT!" where students can read and receive

---

Takeaways

Administrators: For younger learners, much of their education revolves around subject centered content. The premise for this is there are certain areas a learner needs to know before adulthood. Our learners are a group of focused individuals who are coming to higher education with an outcome in mind. Ask yourself, are your processes arbitrary for learners entering the institution? Are they arbitrary for learners attempting to get through to graduation? Stated another way, are there areas where excessive policies or procedures have become barriers to your learners' successes? Most administrators know about problem areas. Sometimes, they don't make sense, but, they exist, so we still use them. Will you attend to these issues?

For those teaching: Learners are no longer on a set path from high school to higher education to a position in the workforce. The skills learners are gaining in the classroom need to be much more about tangible steps they can take to solve real-life issues, rather than a curriculum designed to engage purely in a theoretical discussion. By using real-world events, learners can begin to see the causal connection between classroom material and applying it in their future or current jobs.

Takeaways

Administrators: Motivation is at the heart of the issue, this is true for us, both as facilitators of education, as well as our learners. While we utilize external motivators like free t-shirt giveaways, water bottles, and pizza cutters, we have an opportunity when developing programs to serve our students. By providing opportunities to act on internal motivation we can create critical moments for students to reflect on their growth. This assumption serves to remind us that regardless of where we are in the hierarchy, it's essential for our policies, procedures, and programs to emphasize student development, rather than a quick attempt at high attendance at an event.

For those teaching: The classroom is one of the most potent areas for student growth. A students' ability to truly enjoy education rests in your hands. This isn't designed to scare you, but pulling questions from a test bank, using slideshows from predecessors may get you through the class, but your students will feel the same way. They will do the work to pass, but the desire to learn may be lost when confronted with experiences that emphasize only externally motivating factors or disallow students to pursue their intrinsic motivations. In summation, your class is a gateway to student growth, and that door will only open with proper time, effort, and theory implemented to support learners.

---

a coupon for a free personal pan pizza (BOOK IT, 2019). One of your authors greatly promoted this program as an elementary teacher. After all, it encouraged her students to read books, but, as soon as the external reward went away, so did the students' willingness to read books. Another example is the classroom teacher allowing students to buy items in the 'classroom store' by redeeming good behavior coupons. Parents are also proponents of extrinsic motivation when thy give their child money for good grades or tell the child to perform well at college or they will stop paying for tuition. While some younger students may thrive on external motivation, most post-traditional learners are more internally motivated. Intrinsic motivation is a student's desire to engage in an activity without the need for external pressure. The intrinsic process means students choose their actions such as setting their own goals and participating in self-directed learning. Intrinsically motivated students also control the outcomes they have for learning.

ALLEN TOUGH – SELF-DIRECTED LEARNING

Background

A well-known theory in the post-traditional world, self-directed learning, echoes many of the sentiments of Knowles orientation to learning, in combination with changes in self-concept. Allen Tough (1971) related the idea of self-directed learning in his book *The Adult's Learning Projects: A Fresh Approach to theory and Practice in Adult Learning*. In this book,

Tough (1971) outlined the research he had conducted and shared some exciting concepts for learners. [Note: Society may have different notions of what learning project means now as opposed to the 70's. For our purposes, consider learning projects as a synonym to learning activities.]

Core Concepts

One of the fascinating pieces of his work is the concept of episodes and learning projects. Episodes are "...the foundation on which the definition of a learning project is constructed" (Tough, 1971, p. 7) and is comprised of a way to quantify an activity or intention of a person. In short, if someone sat down for an hour with the intent to read a book, and had a "definite beginning and ending, and is not interrupted for more than two or three minutes by some other activity or purpose" (p. 8) that person would have engaged in an episode. Tough (1971) wrote much about a particular, intentional type of episode called a *learning episode*, which are periods in which "more than half of the person's intention is to gain and retain certain definite knowledge and skill" (p. 8). These learning episodes are at the base of learning projects and give us a tangible way to think about students who direct their learning. To understand and develop criteria for episodes, learning episodes, and learning projects, Tough (1971) engaged in interviews with individuals from seven distinct populations: "blue-collar factory workers, women and men in jobs at the lower end of the white-collar scale, beginning elementary school teachers, municipal politicians, social science professors, and upper-middle-class women with pre-school children" (p. 17). Through these diverse populations, Tough (1971) intended to understand how they engaged in their learning when encountering episodes, learning episodes, and learning projects. Through total hours spent on learning projects, the number of learning projects, and the mean number of hours of each learning project, there were two realizations that became evident. First, there were some clear differences between populations chosen by their occupation, social class, age, sex, and educational level (Tough, 1971). Second, and perhaps more importantly, while these factors did have some effect on total hours, number of projects and mean number of hours, these factors did not fully encapsulate the learner. There were other influential factors, such as "past experiences, current personality or psychological characteristics, the people around him [them], and characteristics of his [their] community and society" (Tough, 1971, p. 22). Understanding the other influential factors is an essential notion for us, as we seek to develop a framework that envelops a learner, provides opportunities, offers a community, and experiences to help students become more engaged in self-directed learning.

Tough's study addresses several points for post-traditional learners. First, the majority of adults have engaged in or are pursuing some self-directed learning (SDL), and that "less than 1% of all the learning projects…were undertaken for credit" (Tough, 1971, p. 19). This means our learners are already consistently engaging in some form of SDL. In comparison, SDL supports Knowles idea of a learner's orientation to learn. Give learners a problem-centered environment that centers on gaining their own knowledge, we should begin to see the intentionality behind the post-traditional learner's desire to engage in this type of learning within a higher education institution.

Furthermore, as we continue to look at how institutions interact with our learners, it's important to note that learners who have used self-directed learning (SDL) not only planned the learning but took responsibility for it. When we consider traditional learners enter from a K-12 environment, frequently there is a sense that many learners are unsure of their path, direction, or how they should focus their time and attention. As such, many of our undergraduate courses reflect this mindset, despite the fact that many higher education institutions have a large population of post-traditional learners in the classroom. We now move on to another theory, one that examines the need for post-traditional learners to design their learning, which touches on learners' sense of self-efficacy as explained by Tinto (2016) and on Knowles' (1980) readiness to learn.

Takeaways

Administrators: Self-concept is a building block that good administrators acknowledge, and account for when developing policies. Learners are major stakeholders at your institution and they will develop internal coalitions with faculty and professional staff if their ability to pursue their educational goals is interrupted. If policies are stifling, learners may decide not to persist, which directly affects the health of the institution.

For those teaching: We agree with Tough that the majority of our learning occurs outside the classroom, yet, less than 1% receive credit for this type of learning. This makes the 1% of learning engagement even more vital. It highlights that learners can engage with content on their own and be masters of their education. Being a master of your education means instructors need to be a guide and support for those who are working through higher education, and understand the important role we play, both as mentors and instructors, as students' grow.

VINCENT TINTO – MODEL OF STUDENT RETENTION

Background

Vincent Tinto (1975) is attributed as one of the first people to synthesize current literature on student retentions/dropouts in his review *Dropout from Higher Education: A Theoretical Synthesis of Recent Research*. This literature review sought to highlight an issue within current literature, and its lack of differentiation between student factors that led to misleading implications (p. 90). Tinto (1975) sought to explain student dropouts, which we now call stopouts, as well as what behaviors, or, risk factors, led to a student leaving a postsecondary institution.

Core Concepts

One of the significant principles put forth by Tinto (1975) was that the "process of dropout from college can be viewed as a longitudinal process of interactions between the individual and the academic and social systems of the college…" (p. 94). Put simply, how we interact with our students can completely change a student's potential to decide to leave higher education. While this may be considered standard ideology and a major function of postsecondary institutions, now, this was a very novel idea less than fifty years ago. It's important to see the timeline of how rapidly we've evolved on this topic in higher education and in modern society. Tinto (1975) also explains what this means for postsecondary institutions, saying "…the model argues that it is the individual's integration into the academic and social systems of the college that most directly relates to his continuance in that college" (p. 96). This emphasis on the institution's role in a student's academic and social systems is still relevant today. Before we move on to these topics, let's dig just a little further. Tinto (1975) went on to define several external factors that influenced learner dropout rates. These included the learner's family background, individual characteristics, past educational experiences, and goal commitment. Let's examine each of these external factors.

Interesting fact: Tinto (1975) built his synthesis of student dropout using Durkheim's theory of suicide. Tinto (1975) noted the similarities between Durkheim's two integration types: insufficient moral integration and insufficient collective affiliation (p. 91).

Learner's Family Background

The learner's background actively contributed to the chance of a learner dropping out at the time of Tinto's (1975) writings. One of the most obvious factors as to whether a student would drop out was the inverse relationship between the family's socioeconomic status and dropout. Families within the "top family income quartile are 8 times more likely to obtain a bachelor's degree by age 24 as compared to individuals from the lowest family income quartile" (American Psychological Association, n.d., p. 2). Additionally, if a family was of lower socioeconomic status, a student's chance of completion in the science, technology, engineering, and math (STEM) disciplines were much lower compared to other students from underrepresented population (American Psychological Association, n.d.). The quoted studies have all occurred within the past five years, making socioeconomic status still a very real issue for our learners today.

Individual Characteristics

While Tinto (1975) explains that standardized tests and previous grades can be somewhat of a predictor, many other varying factors can't be quantified by these measures, which were, and in some cases still, are standards still used to predict student success. Attributes, such as being more "impulsive," as well as lacking "deep emotional commitment to education" and "lack of flexibility" were among many of the attributes linked with learner dropout. The contrast between these attributes and updated models will give you a respectable understanding of how far the focus has evolved since the 1970s.

Past Educational Experience

As we look at current changes in our nation's K-12 education systems, it's prudent to see how the concept of privilege has interacted consistently in the education world. Tinto (1975) outlined that the characteristics of a learner's high school profoundly affect the learner's chance of doing well in higher education. Characteristics of the school include the academic staff, facilities, and how these factors affect a learner's expectations of postsecondary education. In 2019, these factors still exist and continue to add complexity and uniqueness to each learner that we encounter.

Goal Commitment

A learner's commitment, drive, or otherwise intrinsic motivation directly affects a learner's dropout rate. The quantifiable measures of this, such as "educational plans, educational expectations, or career expectations, the higher the level of plans, the more likely the individual is to remain in college" (Tinto, 1975, p. 102). The most interesting of these tangible items is the higher the level of plans, which indicates that our learners who are consistently considering their futures have a better chance of persisting through the demands of postsecondary education.

Each of these characteristics provides a small glimpse, not only into the 1970's culture surrounding student retention. Unlike several of the other theorists, who have since stopped publishing on their respective works, Tinto (2017) has continued to work to update his model, which we'll cover below.

Current Context: Vincent Tinto's Updated Model

While Vincent Tinto's original theory emphasized retention, his updated model reflects a paradigm shift from retention to the idea of learner persistence. Since our book emphasizes factors that would contribute to fulfilling post-traditional learner's needs, learner persistence is worth including. Tinto's (2016) updated model emphasizes three main areas, self-efficacy, sense of belonging, and the curriculum.

Self-efficacy is an essential building block for post-traditional learners. Similar to Knowles (1980) idea of the orientation of the learner, self-efficacy involves a learner's outlook on his or her ability to perform the required task. Post-traditional learners often come into the classroom nervous about their time spent out of school (Bigdeli, 2010). Classes that fulfill the needs of post-traditional undergraduate learners, especially in the first year of study, can help shape a learner's outlook on their self-efficacy (Tinto, 2017). As such, including Tinto's emphasis on self-efficacy, can help to create an inclusive system for learners.

A sense of belonging is the second factor that contributes to learners' persistence. Learners both desire and need to feel like they are a part of a community. This community extends not only from the university but also from other learners (Tinto, 2017). The emphasis on a sense of belonging is

> **Takeaways**
>
> **Administrators:** You can see the stark contrast between Tinto's original works in 1975 as compared to the updated 2017 model. Similar to designing a mission statement for the university, your department, or unit, you should have the idea of student persistence in the back of your mind. Doing so, is a great way to better serve your students and support their growth. Self-concept is a building block that effective administrators acknowledge, and, account for, when developing policies. If policies are stifling, learners may decide not to persist, which directly affects the health of the institution.
>
> **For those teaching:** Many of our strategies revolve around the idea of risk factors and retention. As an instructor, you can influence a learner's sense of belonging, value of the curriculum, and self-efficacy. These are all important concepts that add to learners' overall experience in higher education, as well as motivators for their classroom work. By intentionally designing your curriculum, designing a supportive environment, and allowing learners to feel like they belong in the classroom, you can support your learners in ways that you did not think possible.

another area that universities can directly affect, and the universities' campus and culture heavily influence learners' sense of belonging. As the learners need to feel a part of a community, the community factors into the system. In short, an effective teaching strategy can assist post-traditional learners in their desire for community, because their experience is directly shaped by a learner's interactions with other learners, academics, professional staff and administrators, whether the interactions occur on-campus or online (Tinto, 2017).

The curriculum is the final updated area from Tinto's (2017) work. As learners balance their roles both in and outside of education, the tangibility of the knowledge they're learning is of paramount importance. One of the significant ways to increase persistence is to design material that is both high quality and relevant to a learner's life (Tinto, 2017). Often, many professors teach through a theoretical context, rather than a realistic one (Knowles, 1980). Therefore, higher education curricula should place an equal emphasis on practical curriculum which helps learners apply the theory.

MEZIROW'S TRANSFORMATIVE LEARNING THEORY

Background

Mezirow's (1991) conception of perspective transformation "has become the most studied and written about adult learning theory since Knowles (1980) proposed andragogy in the 1970s" (Merriam, 2014, p. 82). As a theory, the perspective transformation is unique in that its approach has humanistic roots.

Takeaways

Administrators: Mezirow highlights some major transformations that can occur for our learners during their time in postsecondary education. As administrators, there are ways to promote student reflection. Emphasizing mentorship and a desire for reflection help promote reflection within the group. There exists a unique opportunity for learners, including your professionals, to experience a dilemma, and critically assess their current position, all within a safe environment. By offering your instructors professional development that includes ways to better serve students and provoke critical reflection, learners may challenge their existing norms, and build towards the soft skills you want them to have before completing their education.

For those teaching: We'll continue to hammer this idea home but taking a step back and really designing a strong teaching experience that emphasizes learner development will not only help your evaluations, it will provide an experience where learners can challenge their norms, assumptions, and leave your institution with a better worldview than before the class. As with some of the previous sections we've discussed, the format, in which you present your instruction, is up to you. Designing programs with the care and seriousness that is required, do take time, but your and your learners' overall experiences in the classroom will be better.

Core Concepts

Mezirow's (1991) transformative learning involves taking one's experiences and "making meaning" (Merriam, 2014, p. 84) of those experiences. While we typically take our experiences for granted, there are specific events known as a "disorienting dilemma" (Mezirow et al., 2000, p. 22) that completely change our frame of reference. Mezirow et al. (2000) developed a ten-step process which recognizes people pass through several stages, eventually recognizing their discontent can be transformed, and ultimately reintegrating a new frame of reference that supports their newly found perspective. Mezirow et al. (2000) ten step process consists of the following:

1. A disorienting dilemma;
2. Self-examination (with feelings of shame or guilt);
3. A critical assessment of epistemic, sociocultural, or psychic assumptions;
4. Recognition of a connection between one's discontent and the process of transformation;
5. Exploration of options for new roles, relationships, and actions;
6. Planning a course of action;
7. Acquisition of knowledge and skills for implementing one's plan;
8. Provisional trying of new roles;
9. Building of competence and self-confidence in new roles and relationships;
10. A reintegration into one's life on the basis of conditions dictated by one's new perspective. (Roberts, 2013, p. 101)

Post-traditional learners, ages twenty-five or older, lend to Mezirow's theory, as many individuals have encountered some disorienting dilemma that has led to the learner returning to higher education. Post-traditional learners are hungry for knowledge and have a desire and willingness to succeed. When we look at many current higher education policies, learning activities, assessments, and outcomes, we need to examine the value of how shaping our classroom experiences can challenge learners in their worldview and open up opportunities for post-traditional learners to again re-assess their current standpoints surrounding their personal and professional lives.

CHAPTER TWO SUMMARY

Each of the theorists presented, thus far, offers a unique piece of the puzzle to help complete a picture of a post-traditional learners' needs. Here's our summary of each piece of the puzzle.

Through Knowles (1980), we were able to highlight some of the significant assumptions regarding adult learners. Using our definition of post-traditional learners, these learners' assumptions are an excellent guidepost to support them through their higher education journey. Before designing programs, learning activities or assessments, review these assumptions, as they provide a strong base to support post-traditional learner needs.

Based on Tough's (1971) research, we were able to see how learners continue to design and plan their learning, and how these skills can be developed through learner interactions in higher education. By taking pieces from a post-traditional learners' playbook, we can help mirror and model ways to improve a learner's ability to be a lifelong learner. Remember, post-traditional learners are returning for a reason, and understanding how education plays a key role in a learner's life can help when developing policies, activities, and events.

Tinto (1975) helped us see how an administrator's perspective in higher education is changing, and how we can leverage updates to theory to support our learners as they seek to persist through their educational journey. By understanding the complexities that administrators face in the retention realm, and recognizing the needs of post-traditional learners who seek to persist, we can develop both policy and outcomes that better serve the interests of both parties.

Through Mezirow (1991), we saw another take on the way post-traditional learners understand the world. As post-traditional learners work through their current viewpoints, reassess, and readjust from disorienting dilemmas, they can better serve their changing worldviews and, hopefully, become more well-rounded individuals. By leveraging our own understanding of how learners change their frames of reference, we can better support learners' in the classroom to continue to develop these worldviews to become globally engaged and lifelong learners.

The following case study provides an opportunity to consider the theoretical context we've learned about in this chapter. Written from the perspective of both the instructor and chair, consider how you would integrate not only your post-traditional learner information in chapter one, but also the theory you would use as the basis of justification for "Dealing with Disaster".

DEALING WITH DISASTER CASE STUDY

Read the scenario, then choose the perspective you wish to address the issues. The perspectives include the instructor's view; your chair's view, aptly named Dr. Chair, or consider both perspectives.

INSTRUCTOR'S VIEW

Scenario: You've landed a tenure track position at a university. The culture and "fit" of the institution are exceptional, and you're nervously anticipating your first set of classes. The fall semester starts on Monday. Excited, you've been working all summer to prepare courses that engage students with active learning. You've utilized Fink's (2003) integrated course design, along with aspects of Quality Matters and backwards design tips you picked up. You've learned as much as you feel you can about traditional, non-traditional, post-traditional, adult learners, and every different but related term you could master. It's the Friday before the first day of classes begin. You are getting ready to head out of your office when Dr. Chair stops by to ask if you have a minute.

Stepping into the office, you can tell your chair has a grim look on his face. Dr. Chair informs you that Dr. Associate, one of the associate professors at the institution has just been hired by another university, and will leave shortly after the new semester begins. With all of Dr. Associate's advisees, as well as preparation for the semester, Dr. Chairs asks you bluntly, "I'm in a real bind, and I need someone to teach Human Resource Administration this semester, would you do it?"

Before you're able to speak, Dr. Chair continues. "Dr. Associate designed the course, and has shared the previous syllabi for the course with me." Dr. Chair then tells you. "I also have access to the course shell in our learning management system. Would you be able to teach this course for our department? We're short on time, so won't be able to hire a qualified adjunct faculty member in time for the start of classes."

Knowing this would bode well for your relationship with Dr. Chair, and the tenure process, you agree. Dr. Chair beams with happiness, "Excellent! The course meets on Monday nights, from 6-9PM. I'll add you to the course shell and e-mail you the syllabus." Stepping out of the room in a daze, you realize that this new class you're supposed to teach is 73 hours away. You work all weekend to synthesize the information, but human resources is not your main area of expertise. With such a limited amount of time, you decide to rely on the presentation slides and notes available from Dr. Associate.

The first class. Your first class ends as nothing short of a disaster. While the traditional icebreakers went well, and you started to get to know your class, you could feel the dread from students. The learning activities, assessments, and outcomes did not match what you had learned about active learning and seemed to fit in the "remember" area of Bloom's (1971) taxonomy, asking students to recall rather than apply, analyze or create using the content. In short, nothing in the current syllabus seems to fit the needs of your students, and you can tell it on their faces as you end the evening class.

The next morning, Dr. Chairs asks you to step into his office. "I had a couple of students come to me this morning with concerns about the human resources class. Would you like to talk about it?"

Questions to consider:

- How would you approach this conversation?
- Is it a good idea to call out Dr. Associate's teaching style?
- What could you do to readjust the class to better fit students' needs?

Dr. Chair's View

Scenario: You are chair of the department, and have enjoyed a stable department for several years. You're approaching the fifth year under your leadership, with fall classes less than a week away. On the Friday before the semester starts, one of your associate professors, Dr. Associate, has just come to you with some news.

"Dr. Chair, I apologize for meeting with you so late. I've been interviewing at different R1 institutions, and I was just offered a new position at my dream university."

You are visibly taken aback. Dr. Associate has been a stalwart member of your department, specializing in several areas, and has shown no signs of displeasure. You say "I know you've considered joining an R1 institution, but I'll admit I'm a bit surprised. I'm excited you were offered a position, and I can tell you're invested. When did they ask you to start? Spring? Next fall?"

Dr. Associate shifts uncomfortably. Uh oh, you think to yourself. Dr. Associate starts slowly, "They've asked me to come onboard this semester. They just lost one of their senior members, and are looking for a strong member to join the department. I'd like to start with them on Monday." You feel your chest tensing up and can hear you saying to yourself - there's only three days until classes. Dr. Associate teaches three classes and has twenty or so advisees. Logistically, this is a nightmare, but it's clear Dr. Associate is determined to leave. Unsure what to do, you say "Well, I appreciate you letting me know, Dr. Associate. Given the timing of the semester, I need to hurry and make arrangements for this coming semester." Dr. Associate leaves your office, darting down the hallway. As you pass by on your way to another faculty member's office, you can see Dr. Associate's office is almost completely cleared out.

You review Dr. Associate's list of advisees and classes for this semester, and clearly, you have some hard decisions to make. Your own load is heavy with teaching two classes, thirty advisees at the masters and doctoral level, plus all of your administrative duties. There's no possible way for you to teach three more classes and another twenty advisees. This would be unmanageable for you considering your current load.

Reflective questions to consider if you were Dr. Chair:

- Would you, and, if so, how would you break up the workload of advisees and classes?

- Do you add these classes to your other existing professors' loads and risk burnout?
- As the chair, is there a feasible amount for you to add to your existing load? What about your work-life balance?

DR. CHAIR'S DECISION

You decide you can push back a couple of projects you hoped to complete in the semester. This allows you to feasibly take on two of the classes, but a third would be too much. Considering Dr. Associates' advisees, you are the most qualified to take them. By taking on the majority of the course and advisee load, you decide it would be less disruptive for the department. Figuring out what to do with the final class is your primary goal. You have a recently hired assistant professor who is teaching three classes for you but has a minimum advisee list. You bring that person into the office.

You explain to your assistant professor that Dr. Associate has just been hired by another university and is leaving immediately to teach for them. With all of Dr. Associate's advisees, as well as preparation for the semester, you are unable to teach the final class, and ask bluntly, "I'm in a real bind, and I need someone to teach Human Resource Administration this semester, would you do it?"

Sensing concern about the work involved three days before class, you continue. "Dr. Associate designed the course and has shared the previous syllabi for the course with me. I also have access to the course shell in our learning management system. Would you be able to teach this course for me? We're short on time, and I won't be able to hire a qualified adjunct faculty member in time."

Your assistant professor agrees to take over the class, letting you breathe a sigh of relief as you to head into the weekend. Between the new advisees and the new classes, as well as some changes on campus, you're going to have your hands very full this semester.

The following Tuesday, one of your graduate assistants asks if you have a free minute. Expecting the usual "what do you need done this week," you instead hear, "I'm not sure I want to take Human Resource Administration this semester, is there something else I can take?" You're taken aback by this statement, your graduate assistant has never approached you regarding taking a different class. Putting your advisor hat on, you ask a couple of open-ended questions. "Tell me more. Is there something regarding the class that doesn't interest you?" She seems fidgety and nervous but eventually tells you "The class is bad. Really bad. Probably one of the worst I've had. The professor is disorganized, and the way we will be assessed makes me nervous. It's all quizzes and tests. I have a lot of test anxiety, and I don't think it would be good for me." You assure your graduate assistant that you will look further into this and ask your instructor to meet with you later that morning.

Questions to consider:

- As you prepare for the meeting, what types of supportive comments should you consider?
- How would you approach this conversation?

REFERENCES

American Psychological Association. (n.d.). *Education and socioeconomic status*. Retrieved from https://www.apa.org/pi/ses/resources/publications/factsheet-education.pdf

Association of American Colleges & Universities. (2015, January 20). *Employers judge recent graduates ill-prepared for today's workplace, endorse broad and project-based learning as best preparation for career opportunity and long-term success*. Retrieved from http://www.aacu.org/press/press-releases/2015employerlearnersurveys

Bigdeli, S. (2010). Affective learning: The anxiety construct in adult learners. *Procedia: Social and Behavioral Sciences*, *9*, 674–678. doi:10.1016/j.sbspro.2010.12.216

Bloom, B. S. (1971). Mastery learning. In J. H. Block (Ed.), *Mastery learning: Theory and practice*. New York: Holt, Rinehart & Winston.

Bye, D., Pushkar, D., & Conway, M. (2007). Motivation, Interest, and Positive Affect in Traditional and Nontraditional Undergraduate Students. *Adult Education Quarterly*, *57*(2), 141–158. doi:10.1177/0741713606294235

Donaldson, J. F., & Graham, S. (1999). A Model of College Outcomes for Adults. *Adult Education Quarterly*, *50*(1), 24–40. doi:10.1177/074171369905000103

Freeman, S., Eddy, S., Mcdonough, M., Smith, M., Nnadozie, O., Jordt, H., & Wenderoth, M. (2014). Active learning increases student performance in science, engineering, and mathematics. *Proceedings of the National Academy of Sciences of the United States of America, 111*(23), 8410–8415. doi:10.1073/pnas.1319030111 PMID:24821756

Knowles, M. (1980). The modern practice of adult education: From pedagogy to andragogy. New York, NY: Cambridge.

Merriam, S. B., & Bierema, L. L. (2014). *Adult learning: Linking theory and practice* (Kindle Edition). Retrieved from Amazon.com

Mezirow, J. (1991). *Transformative dimensions of adult learning.* San Francisco, CA: JosseyBass.

Mezirow, J., & ... (2000). *Learning as transformation: Critical perspectives on a theory in progress.* San Francisco, CA: Jossey-Bass.

Roberts, N. (2013). *Disorienting dilemmas: Their effects on learners, impact on performance, and implications for adult educators.* Retrieved from https://digitalcommons.fiu.edu/cgi/viewcontent.cgi?referer=https://www.google.com/&httpsredir=1&article=1249&context=sferc

Tinto, V. (1975). Dropout from Higher Education: A Theoretical Synthesis of Recent Research. *Review of Educational Research, 45*(1), 89–125. doi:10.3102/00346543045001089

Tinto, V. (2016, September 26). From retention to persistence. *Inside Higher Ed.* Retrieved from https://www.insidehighered.com/views/2016/09/26/how-improve-student-persistence-and-completion-essay

Tough, A. (1971). *The adult's learning projects: A fresh approach to theory and practice in adult learning.* Toronto: Ontario Institute for Studies in Education.

Tsai, C. Y., Li, Y. Y., & Cheng, Y. Y. (2016). The Relationships Among Adult Affective Factors, Engagement in Science, and Scientific Competencies. *Adult Education Quarterly, 67*(1), 30–47. doi:10.1177/0741713616673148

Wang, V. X. (2014). *Advanced Research in Adult Learning and Professional Development: Tools.* Trends, and Methodologies. doi:10.4018/978-1-4666-4615-5

Chapter 3
Learning Approaches and You

ABSTRACT

In this chapter, the authors will outline several learning approaches. Each learning approach will have a base summary followed by the context that the approach can be utilized when working with post-traditional learners. After the initial summaries and takeaways, the authors will delve into a learning approach framework they have designed surrounding social constructivism. Finally, the authors provide several case studies to consider the learned content. Each case study includes prompts for instructors and administrators.

INTRODUCTION

In the preceding chapters, you were provided with overviews of several theories. The overviews included initial takeaways and case studies to help you make sense of the material. We believe this background information will help you feel comfortable enough to add new perspectives to your learning.

To break up the monotony of theory after theory, here are a few of our favorite sayings from instructors and administrators.

If it's not broke, don't fix it.

We've always done it this way.

That's not our department's policy.

DOI: 10.4018/978-1-7998-0145-0.ch003

Copyright © 2020, IGI Global. Copying or distributing in print or electronic forms without written permission of IGI Global is prohibited.

When we say "favorite" we really mean "detrimental to learner success". Often, our work updating policies or programs is stifled by this logic. While there is merit in consistency and explicitness, there is just as much merit in utilizing theory and new research to support your learners. You may be thinking that you've learned more than your fair share of the different theories discussed in the previous chapters. In some ways, you're right. You could take the first two chapters and immediately start to implement new and revised policies and programs. However, to take your policies and programs to the next level, there is another element that can really serve as the foundation for success in your work. That element is learning frameworks. You will be surprised to know that understanding a few essential learning frameworks, such as the Constructivist and Behaviorist approaches, will maximize the previously discussed theoretical concepts to help you interact with and personalize the learning approaches. These frameworks serve as pathways for you to consider when designing your learning. Each framework's beliefs are very different and these approaches to learning will dictate where you naturally place your attention when designing activities. Each framework, we will discuss, reveals a different approach to the same problem but is useful when considering both your colleagues' perspectives, as well as your learners' perspectives. Understanding your use of each learning framework, allows you to explore other ways people interact with knowledge, check your own assumptions, and create a more cohesive approach to designing policies, procedures, and teaching materials. There's little doubt that you have a tendency for a framework, whether you have been introduced to it or not. As you continue to read, reflect which of the learning frameworks resonate with you the most then consider how the other frameworks could benefit your approaches to learning and working with colleagues and students.

This chapter overviews the Positivist, Constructivist, Postmodern, Humanistic, and Behaviorist perspectives. Each learning framework will include:

1. A summary of the learning approach,
2. A well-known theory or concept resulting from the approach,
3. Notable theorists and additional references, and
4. Takeaways for instructors and administrators.

Behaviorism

There are several ways to quantify learning. While each of the frameworks has their own take on how learning is changing the person, there are some interesting philosophical notions that come at learning from different angles. When considering Behaviorism, one of the easiest ways we've found to describe behavioral change in learners is through the field of counseling. In counseling, whether mental health or drug counseling, you seek to make a change in a learner's behavior. If you know of or have been to counseling before, there is consistent work to reduce maladjustments while increasing positive behavior. (Counseling does much more than that, but it's a good place to start.). As you read through the main points, consider this framework from a counseling perspective.

Main Points

Behaviorism says that "learning is a change in behavior" (Merriam, 2014, p. 26). In behaviorism, learning consists of using behavioral objectives, and how those behaviors are judged (Merriam, 2014). As a professor, behaviorism occurs with the learning objectives, as well as "quantifiable, systematic, and observable outcomes…" (Merriam, 2014, p. 27). By using the mechanics of observable outcomes in the classroom, specifically through expected behaviors for learners, as well as rubrics and scaffolding, learners measure up or perform to the agreed upon standard.

Notable Theorists – Pavlov, Skinner, Watson

For those who have any background in psychology, you've probably heard of Ivan Pavlov, B.F. Skinner, and John Watson.

Pavlov's Classical Conditioning

Ivan Pavlov (1910) is famous for his emphasis on classical conditioning. By linking stimuli together, a person can develop a learned response. Pavlov tested his theory on dogs, in which he paired a sound with incoming food.

Note: We will use several different words interchangeably to describe learning approaches. If you see perspective, approach, lens or framework, we're still referring to the core idea of interacting with learning approaches.

Pavlov noticed that dogs would salivate before eating, and hypothesized that if he played a tone before the dogs ate, he would be able to elicit salivation from the dogs. Lo and behold, it worked. After several instances of pairing the sound with food, the dogs would start to salivate, even if no food was present. This paved the way for classical conditioning and became the catalyst for a very ethically, murky experiment conducted by John Watson.

Waston and Little Albert

John Watson is famous for a test he performed, called the "Little Albert Experiment" (Watson & Rayner, 1920). This experiment involved an eleven-month-old male infant. The infant was exposed to several different stimuli, including most notably a rat. When exposed to the rat, the infant showed no fear but was introduced to a loud banging noise after encountering the rat. While the child did not initially cry near the rat, he would cry after the banging noise. The paired stimuli were consistently introduced until the child would start to cry upon seeing the rat, thus showing the child was aware of the loud banging that would be introduced. This showed that behavior can be elicited by pairing stimuli, and pushed forth the view that behavior can be changed in humans.

Skinner and Operant Conditioning

Burrhus Frederic Skinner or B. F. Skinner (1938) is well known for Operant Conditioning. Unlike Watson, Skinner believed there was more to the equation than merely pairing stimuli. Skinner found that your behavior could be modified in several ways, and came up with three major points that occur after a response. The first, *Neutral Operants*, saw responses that neither increased nor diminished a behavior. In short, the stimuli did not change much. The second, *Reinforcers*, did precisely as the name implies. The stimuli would reinforce the chance that the behavior could occur. Finally, P*unishers* decreased the likelihood that the behavior would continue to happen (Skinner, 1938). With each of these response types, Skinner attempted to point out that there were ways for learners to be pushed towards or away from eliciting a specific kind of behavior.

Looking at current society, there are instances of operant conditioning occurring everywhere. At the beginning of the fall semester on many college campuses, there is an influx of activity in the parking lots. When you park in

> **Wrapping your head around the Behaviorist perspective.** Think about the Behaviorist perspective for a moment. If we can elicit responses from learners, then it can be argued they have learned from that paired stimuli. But how does the elicited response fit into a person's current worldview and context? Did the ability to elicit a response cause the learner to truly "learn"? Let's consider the No Child Left Behind (NCLB) Act, enacted in 2001. On the surface, this act looked to help disadvantaged students and create equal education for students. In fact, the program led to behaviors that initially seemed to support the notion that NCLB could be successful (U.S. Department of Education, 2014). Standardized test scores in some areas directly increased, which means the program was successful…right? The issue with NCLB was, for many instructors, they reached a point where they felt they were "teaching to the test," rather than emphasizing application or critical thinking of the material. Theoretically, the learners learned the content, since their scores increased on the standardized tests. However, if the emphasis is on only being able to recognize content for a test, does this indicate the learner synthesized the material? This is where sharp criticism occurs for Behaviorism, which makes it too deterministic, and disallows freedom of choice. [We put forth an argument later that, while this may be an appropriate mechanism to teach a practical skill, it may not provide the depth necessary to support a learner's synthesis of all material].

the wrong lot on campus during this influx, you receive a warning ticket (A shout out to everyone who has received one of these.). This is an example of campus safety trying to modify your behavior. Providing a warning intends to act as a light punisher, causing you to park in the correct parking lot, while still allowing some latitude, the intended outcome of the warning ticket is to instill the 'correct' behavior in you.

POSITIVISM AND POST-POSITIVISM

Main Points - Positivist Perspective

The Positivist perspective emphasizes cause and effect and verified data. It includes "the elements of being reductionistic, logical, empirical, cause-and-effect oriented, and deterministic based on a priori theories" (Creswell & Poth, 2018, p. 68). When working with someone, or, if this is the view you subscribe to, a positivist believes that there is a solid answer to each question. For those who seek to live in a world of yes or no, this perspective is usually suited in the direction of their needs. In our experiences, we've found that health-related or STEM professionals may lean toward this perspective. As a perspective, the Positivist may have unwavering faith that each problem is solvable, but this faith receives criticism because there isn't an answer to every problem. Should there be an answer to every problem? To deal with the criticism of the Positivist perspective, some people, who identified as Positivists, are now choosing to embrace the Postpositivist movement.

Bonus! (Everyone loves that, right?). Bandura (1977) puts forth a theory that helps mend some of the deterministic issues presented in earlier Behavioristic approaches. In Bandura (1977) Social Learning Theory, it is through the Behaviorist perspective that we can learn new behaviors without needing to act ourselves. "Traditional theories of learning generally depict behavior as the product of directly experienced response consequences. In actuality, virtually all learning phenomena resulting from direct experiences can occur on a vicarious basis through observation of other people's behavior and its consequences for them" (p. 2).

Takeaways for administrators – Post-traditional learners are entering higher education with behaviors learned in other roles. These behaviors differ from learner to learner, but some post-traditional learners "require developmental education to be successful in college-level courses" (Soares, 2013, p. 2). As we consider courses required for curriculums, as well as the programs, events, and policies we propose, particular emphasis should be placed on providing post-traditional learners with comprehensive courses and support such as tutoring, counseling, and academic advising sessions.

Takeaways for instructors – Post-traditional learners have a lot to offer in the classroom. Their outside knowledge, experience, and expertise allows them to provide unique perspectives in the classroom. As instructors, our understanding of reinforcers and punishers can be a gift or a curse for our post-traditional learners. As you develop your policies surrounding expectations in your course, including late policies and attendance, take special consideration of the language you select when developing group or peer discussions and implementing standards. Allowing learners to share their previous experiences in a safe space can help to set a standard for learners. Using reinforcers to support learners through feedback is also a must, as it allows learners to feel validated and increases their self-efficacy.

Main Points - Postpositivist Perspective

A major and conspicuous issue with the Positivist perspective is the absolute belief in solutions, and that cause and effect governs this realm. Postpositivists recognize this issue, and "…do not believe in strict cause and effect but rather recognize that all cause and effect is a probability that may or may not occur" (Creswell and Poth, 2018, p. 68).

Notable Theorists – Kuhn, Popper

Thomas Kuhn

While there are many notable theorists of both Positivist and Postpositivist perspectives, we're going to delve more deeply into the Postpositivist perspective. Thomas Kuhn (1962) is a large contributor to the Postpositivist movement, and we believe this quote aptly illustrates Kuhn's radical thought process.

The more carefully they study, say, Aristotelian dynamics, phlogistic chemistry, or caloric thermodynamics, the more certain they feel that those once current views of nature were, as a whole, neither less scientific nor more the product of human idiosyncrasy than those current today. If these

---

An <u>excerpt</u> from Karl Popper's Science: Conjectures and Refutations

These considerations led me in the winter of 1919-20 to conclusions which I may now reformulate as follows.

(1) It is easy to obtain confirmations, or verifications, for nearly every theory-if we look for confirmations.

(2) Confirmations should count only if they are the result of risky predictions; that is to say, if, unenlightened by the theory in question, we should have expected an event which was incompatible with the theory--an event which would have refuted the theory.

(3) Every 'good' scientific theory is a prohibition: it forbids certain things to happen. The more a theory forbids, the better it is.

(4) A theory which is not refutable by any conceivable event is nonscientific. Irrefutability is not a virtue of a theory (as people often think) but a vice.

(5) Every genuine test of a theory is an attempt to falsify it, or to refute it. Testability is falsifiability; but there are degrees of testability: some theories are more testable, more exposed to refutation, than others; they take, as it were, greater risks.

(6) Confirming evidence should not count except when it is the result of a genuine test of the theory; and this means that it can be presented as a serious but unsuccessful attempt to falsify the theory. (I now speak in such cases of 'corroborating evidence'.)

(7) Some genuinely testable theories, when found to be false, are still upheld by their admirers--for example by introducing ad hoc some auxiliary assumption, or by re-interpreting the theory ad hoc in such a way that it escapes refutation. Such a procedure is always possible, but it rescues the theory from refutation only at the price of destroying, or at least lowering, its scientific status. (I later described such a rescuing operation as a 'conventionalist twist' or a 'conventionalist stratagem'.) One can sum up all this by saying that the criterion of the scientific status of a theory is its falsifiability, or refutability, or testability. (Popper, 1963, p. 7)

---

out-of-date beliefs are to be called myths, then myths can be produced by the same sorts of methods and held for the same sorts of reasons that now lead to scientific knowledge. If, on the other hand, they are to be called science, then science has included bodies of belief quite incompatible with the ones we hold today. (Kuhn, 1962, p. 2)

As a theorist, Kuhn (1962) understood the emphasis placed on mere cause and effect belied the true reality facing Positivists, that regardless of their attempts to withhold the human element, our current view of the world will change, and we can only emphasize our current views, with the understanding that they will continue to change. This led to the Postpositivist views that Kuhn espouses; that the work we do is not tied to only cause and effect, but rather there is a possibility of changes to occur. We'll call this the human element.

Karl Popper

Karl Popper (1963) was another important Postpositivist. Part of the reason we included Popper was to highlight conclusions he believed were correct in his 1963 book. These conclusions help to explain and emphasize how the Positivist and the Postpositivist perspectives differ and the interaction amongst the two theories.

Karl Popper's (1963) interpretation of the way theory is presented, and specifically how a theory must be shaped in order to stand up to a scientific status leads us to the interesting idea of how we engage with our learners in the classroom or through our policies. While we may not establish a theory, the criteria still stand as a reasonable belief to consider when developing our policies, procedures, and instruction. Are the methods we invoke tested? Do the learning activities, outcomes and assessments provide learners with the gains they need? Or, do each of the activities, outcomes, and assessments simply confirm what we believe, and then move on? Let's use our example of the Common Core curriculum, while the curriculum may be testable, as it is each time standardized testing is used, again, we ask, does the curriculum embody what we wish our learners should know? These questions continue to lead toward a common thread; the human element in all of this.

Constructivism

One of the most intriguing aspects of this approach is the emphasis on understanding the current world through your own lens. This approach is going to underpin the model we put forth and provides a solid framework for those working in higher education.

Notable theorists – Bruner, Dewey, Piaget

When speaking of Constructivism, there are several notable theorists to examine. John Dewey is credited with designing the main theoretical approach to Constructivism; however, in this book, we prefer to focus more on recent work that highlights advances made in this learning approach. If you're looking to gain more insight into the origins of Constructivism, read through Dewey's original work cited in this chapter. Bruner and Piaget's work are two other helpful sources to use for a comprehensive view on Cognitive Constructivism.

Takeaways for administrators – The most significant takeaway from this perspective is that we can continuously find confirmation for our perceptions. In this current age of news, we're sure you can find a familiar news channel or paper and find validation for all items you consider to be correct. As administrators, we need to be constantly wary of this type of behavior and consistently check our beliefs at the door when we start working on policies and procedures and in our interactions with post-traditional learners. An emphasis on assessment is a good first step, as it allows for consistent engagement on whether the policies, programming and procedures are testable.

Takeaways for instructors – This is one of the few times our takeaways are similar for both administrators and instructors. Instructors need to be wary of searching for confirmation when it comes to learning activities, outcomes, and assessments. It can be easy to write off a learner's complaint as simply a response from someone disgruntled, but to do so means a refusal to assess the issue the learner had. While instructors generally receive evaluations at the end of their course, checking in with learners during the course is never a bad idea. By opening a line of communication, potential issues that may be written off later could be addressed and help to further improve the instruction learners' receive.

As previously mentioned, for our teacher-readers, we prefer to focus on a more recent work about Constructivism, one by Alesandrini and Larson (2002). To apply one of our reoccurring themes of applicability, this work serves as a respectable guidepost for how instructors view Constructivism in the common day and age. There are several areas, in this work, where we want to direct your attention. First "learning results from exploration and discovery" (Alesandrini and Larson, 2002, p. 118). As an instructor, post-traditional learners are looking at you to facilitate a process of exploration and discovery. This process is much easier to accomplish when employing active learning techniques, which is summed up by Alesandrini and Larson (2002) when they state, "instead, teachers in a constructivist classroom are called to function as facilitators who coach learners as they blaze their own paths toward personally meaningful goals" (p. 118). For us, this is a powerful statement. Teachers facilitate the environment and learners create meaning through their own active learning. Earlier in this chapter, each theory that we brought forth, illustrated that learners are taking active steps toward their learning. This learning occurs inside the classroom but, outside the classroom as well, as learners make their own meaning.

Another interesting concept from the more modern Constructivist era is the concept of learning has changed. When we traditionally think of learning, we want someone to have a thorough knowledge of the subject or content before jumping into application. Alesandrini and Larson (2002) state "rather than requiring an understanding *before* applying that understanding to the construction of something, students in the constructivist classroom learn concepts *while* exploring their application" (p. 118). If we're being honest, theoretical concepts reign in many classrooms, across numerous departments in higher education, and throughout entire institutions. For higher education institutions, these theoretical applications have been the bedrock of our teaching for many years. Institutions' introductory and developmental courses surround these concepts. A helpful illustration is to think about an Introduction to College Algebra course, where you're learning important concepts in a theoretical context rather than in a real-world application context.

Social Constructivist

Social Constructivist viewpoints differ slightly than Constructivism in the way the world is viewed. Subscribers to this perspective "develop subjective meaning of their experiences - meanings directed toward certain objects or things" (Creswell & Poth, 2018, p. 69). These meanings become especially important in consideration of our post-traditional learners, who have been exposed to many more roles in their lives, such as parents or wage earners. The multiplicity of these roles creates a new context for learners to consider and provides our post-traditional learners with more reasons to consider the world from a social constructivist view.

Notable Theorists – Vygotsky

Putting it all Together; Learning Redefined

As we examine these prior theories and our own teaching, consider the following quote:

At this point, without a unifying theory as to how the different learning theories interact within a single individual to produce behavior, we have to study these different viewpoints independently and then piecemeal them together into a school curriculum. However, acceptance of a particular viewpoint provides a different starting point for curriculum development. (Huitt, 2009, p.1)

We will now put forth a theoretical model that encompasses the interactions between the varied learning approaches.

Cook's Model of Learning Interactions

We've arrived to a point in this chapter where new information will be posited. This point is a new approach to a theoretical context that describes how you, we, and everyone can apply the different learning approaches. After spending years with hundreds and hundreds of learners from different backgrounds, whether in the education field or in other settings, there are several assumptions that dominate the field of learning and its approaches. We will explicitly state these dominate assumptions and suggest guidelines that are intended to increase the chances of producing the behaviors we truly seek in our learners. It's important to note that this new information is

---

Note: As much as we've been preaching the need for a practical approach, there is absolutely merit in the process of working with and using theories. Cook's Model of Learning Interaction is created based on former theories. Most of life revolves around practicality and applicability, and thus we should emphasize these notions first.

conceptual in nature. To provide a broader context to learning approaches, any new information must be tested and the results used to re-design the rules and assumptions.

Fundamental Rules of Learning Approach Interactions

One of the challenges in higher education is finding ways to merge the knowledge of multiple fields. We often silo ourselves at work specifically with "like people" or "that one person" we know in the other department. What follows is a theoretical basis of rules for learning approach interactions. We put forth the following assumptions and rules regarding the interaction of learning approaches and the suggested impact of these assumptions in the context of higher education learning:

Assumption #1 - Learner theories are all small parts to a bigger picture of learner engagement. Each part has a unique place within education, but these places are context-dependent and are still subject to the following rules.

Rule #1 - The context of the field will dictate the most viable approach.

Rule #2 - While each approach is useful, no approach fits all situations.

Rule #3 - Learning approaches are subject to the base nature of both the instructor as well as the learners.

Rule #4 - Learning approaches are subject to the current social context of both the instructor as well as the learners.

Assumption #2 - Learning is an innately social action, and thus social context dictates how well an approach is viewed by learners, which, in turn, affects learners' motivations and responses to material in the classroom.

Assumption #3 – The amount of time a learner has to learn the material directly affects the response toward learning approaches.

Assumption #4 – The learner's degree of soft skills development directly affects the learner's response toward specific learning approaches.

Let's turn our attention to an examination of each assumption for a more thorough understanding.

Assumption #1 - Learner theories are all small parts to a bigger picture of learner engagement. Each part has a unique place within education, but these places are context dependent.

Theoretical Background

One of the most frustrating aspects about learning approaches is the lack of cohesion between learning approaches. With their existing fundamental rules, rectifying an agreement between these approaches and finding common ground has been a large center of debate in the education community. For those of you with background in business, you may have encountered the concept of positional bargaining or the "you versus me". We don't advocate this type of bargaining, but realize there are some who would disagree. In fact, the view of positional bargaining complements each learning approach, that is, proponents of the learning approaches believe their approach is correct in their assumptions of human behavior.

How did we move away from the positional bargaining lens to approach these assumptions? How did we rectify this continual problem? As with any problem that doesn't have a solution, we turned toward things that *did* have a solution. When speaking on positional bargaining, one of the ways to better negotiate is to focus on interests, not positions. Fisher and Ury (2011) posit some great advice for focusing on interests, saying "the basic problem in a negotiation lies not in conflicting positions, but in the conflict between each side's needs, desires, concerns, and fears" (Location No. 970). As we consider learning approaches, one characteristic that appears to leap out from each theory is the theme of 'you're not correct in your assumptions, here is what's right'. As we know from our own lives, further scrutiny, especially when it comes to human behavior, may end up causing more issues than offering solutions. To avoid this positional bargaining and being rooted in a single position, we instead asked: "Porque no los dos?" (Why not both?). All of the learning approaches have been tested, and are accurate based on their own assumptions, and, thus, each of these current learning approaches is viable to use from an educational standpoint. With this supposition in mind, we move to what we know to be fact, while still maintaining the flexibility for new learning approaches.

Rule #1 - The Context of the Field will Dictate the Most Viable Approach

As we sought to develop rules to apply for the learning approaches, one of the first problems we needed to solve was understanding the interaction between learning approaches and education. Because of the innate social context we live in, there is no best practice or one true approach that will work in all fields. Instead, we find that certain fields will gravitate toward certain learning approaches. Gravitating toward a certain learning approach can be due to multiple factors, including:

1) The vocational positions in the field heavily rely on a specific theorist or type of learning approach, i.e., a drug counseling degree may use more behaviorist learning approaches due to the preferred outcome being a behavioral change.
2) The current 'best practice' or 'high impact practice' research heavily dictates how departments teach their learners, i.e., Freeman et al. (2014) published an article showing student gains in STEM using active learning techniques which may lead to redesigns for many progressive universities.

Rule #2 - While each Approach is Useful, no Approach fits all Situations

As we outlined in earlier chapters, post-traditional learners' needs are different than traditional learners needs. How then, can we seek to claim that one approach is genuinely best when the learner needs change over their lifetime? In short, we cannot rectify this position while maintaining there is a difference in those needs.

Rule #3 - Learning Approaches are Subject to the Base Nature of both the Instructor as well as the Learners

As outlined in this chapter, we stated that instructors and learners have preferred approaches they may naturally gravitate toward. There are natural differences in the way people perceive the world, and thus learning approaches will have a different effect on different individuals. Because of this, all learning approaches are subject to an instructor's natural tendencies toward an approach and are subject as well to the learners in the classroom. While approaches may be successful despite these differences, the depth of their success can depend on the instructors and their learners' willingness to engage in that learning approach.

Rule #4 - Learning Approaches are Subject to the Current Social Context of both the Instructor as well as the Learners

One of the easiest ways to explain the universal application of this rule is to note a time when higher education could not control the pressures being exerted on it. With the advent of disruptive technology, which made its way into higher education over the past fifty years, the higher education landscape does not look the same as it did fifty years ago. Changes in technology have led to an outcry from both internal and external stakeholders, which have forced institutions to change and adopt new approaches to education. The same can be said for instructors. When you look for viable candidates on campus, do you look for someone with technological expertise? Is the ability to use statistical software advantageous to a prospective applicant? Our instructors and the skills we use to teach them in graduate school should have changed to match the growing social demand for technology competent individuals.

Assumption #2 - Learning is an innately social action, and thus social context dictates how well an approach is viewed by learners, which, in turn, affect learners' motivations and responses to material in the classroom.

We want to take you back to your K-12 education for this assumption. Do you remember the main approach your teachers used to help you learn math? Have you seen the "new math" that is being taught in K-12 curriculum now? How about the Common Core curriculum that has been at the center of debate for several years now? Each of these modifications causes a ripple in the education chain and impacts the way our learners view education. Also, outside forces such as economic, political and social forces, drive our learners to adopt assumptions that positively or negatively affect the way they view certain approaches, as well as what they expect in the classroom.

Assumption #3 – The amount of time a learner has to learn the material directly affects the response toward learning approaches.

This assumption can be viewed in two ways. First, it can be viewed as the overall time to achieve the learning via the course length. Second, it can be viewed as the length of time each of our learners has to dedicate to their education. When we put this in the context of post-traditional learners, there are multiple competing priorities from other roles that take up the learners' time. These competing priorities may come from within their role as a learner, in the form of a thesis, final project, dissertation, or perhaps another class. All of this context exerts pressure on a learner and may prevent one specific learning approach from being as effective as we would like it to be.

Assumption #4 – The learner's degree of soft skills development directly affects their response toward specific learning approaches.

This is the final assumption we sought to create surrounding a learner's ability to engage with the material. Indeed, age and experience do play a part in how well a learner can work with multiple learning approaches, but we all have met learners who are wise beyond their years, and able to pick up material regardless of the learning approach. Seeking to rectify how this was possible, we decided to focus on the necessary skills to be successful in any learning approach. Those skills point to what are generally deemed as soft skills, such as communication ability, critical thinking ability, and the ability to work independently. When we examine learners, based on their soft skills development, we tend to find learners, who are more advanced in their soft skill development, generally perform better in a wide range of activities and thus can respond better to different learning approaches. If a learner is juggling work, family, and multiple classes, and feels exhausted before coming to class, the instructor may find it much more difficult to engage that learner with teaching methods rooted in a Constructivist approach.

Chapter Three Conclusion

Learning frameworks are a guidepost to post-traditional learner success. By understanding each of the different frameworks, as well as our newly put forth assumptions, learners at your institution will prosper. While we joked at the beginning of the chapter about people saying, "We've always done it this way." there is merit in examining the way your programs, policies, and teaching interact with these learning frameworks. The following is a case study centered on administrative policy and procedures. Through this case study, consider the learning frameworks, how they can be used for learner growth, as well as for development of potential new policies or procedures.

Administrative Case Study: Greek life and Hazing; North Island Marine University

Note: This and the other case studies presented in the book are fictitious.

North Island Marine University (NIMU) is a small, private institution with roughly 1,500 students. Situated on a small island off the coast of Hawaii, NIMU boasts the proud status of being in *Lifetime Leader's Digest* "Top 10 Prettiest College Campuses in America". While NIMU uses *Lifetime Leader's Digest* as a talking point for parents, NIMU is infamous for another talking point, its higher alcohol consumption. Three years ago, the Bluffington Coast, a well-recognized national newspaper named NIU as #2 in their "Top Five Party Schools" ranking. While NIU is well known for its Marine Biology program, the party school ranking causes NIU to attract two very different types of student. Many students come to pursue NIU's top tier biology programs. However, other students enter due to the party culture at the institution.

While the institution is no stranger to issues with partying and drinking, Ellen Vauss, the Director of Greek Life, has noticed an increasingly problematic trend with her students. Two years ago, Greek Life students held the highest overall GPA of any group on campus and were one of the largest participating teams in volunteer activities on the island. As of her most recent report, though, Greek Life students had slipped dramatically in all chapters, in both GPA and volunteering. Understanding the drinking culture at NIU, and having no turnover within the department, Ellen believes that part of the issue could be a nearby liquor store that opened a year and a half ago, which boasts being open 24 hours a day. Prior to this store opening, most liquor stores closed around 9 p.m. on the island. With her house situated only a block away, Ellen has seen students coming in and out of the liquor store almost every night of the week.

The next day, Ellen consults with her staff regarding student GPA and volunteering tendencies and sets a plan to assess whether alcohol is the issue, or whether there are other issues. After the meeting, Ellen consults with Dr. Patricia Wodd, the Assistant Vice President of Student Affairs about student grades and her thoughts on the liquor store. Dr. Wodd recommends Ellen wait until her assessment is complete before acting and warns her not to take any drastic actions. Without evidence, the town and gown issues (relationship between the community and university) caused could be tremendous, and Greek life at NIU is well known nationally. Begrudgingly, Ellen agrees and moves with her team to assess the Greek Life issue, leaving the 24-hour liquor store issue alone.

A week later, Ellen gets an emergency call from campus security. A party in Zeta Zeta Beta, one of the sanctioned fraternities on campus, was broken up, and several students were found unconscious. These students were shirtless, drawn on, and had their hand's duct taped to two forty-ounce bottles of beer. While campus safety acted quickly and helped many students, one of the students suffered a seizure due to alcohol poisoning, and doctors ruled he has permanent brain damage.

With local papers publishing the story, the national news also picked up the story. With all the negative press, Ellen finds herself in a whirlwind of meetings. NIU's board of directors, the president, and several parents all request meetings to voice their concerns on the matter. Representatives from the national office of Zeta Zeta Beta also call Ellen, and publicly denounce the chapter, ending their status with them. By the end of the week, the president temporarily suspends Greek life on campus, pending an internal investigation.

Ellen is admittedly frustrated. Before the incident, she documented and brought up issues to the assistant vice president, who is now keeping her at a distance. As other chapters were temporarily shut down, Ellen struggles to figure out her next options for the Greek community.

The following Monday morning the office is quiet. Both of Ellen's coordinators barely speak at their meeting, and it's clear that the office believes this shutdown won't be temporary. A few concerned Greek students stop by, but, for the most part, chapters also seem to have resigned themselves to their fate. Ruffling through papers after the team meeting, Ellen receives a phone call. It's Karen Engram, one of the members of the Board of Directors.

"Ellen, I've had several volunteer organizations in the community call requesting more information about the temporarily shut down. It seems several volunteers are decrying our shutdown, citing how essential Greek life is to the surrounding community with their commitment to volunteering. Do you think we could set up a meeting for tomorrow?"

Ellen is excited. This is the first piece of public support she's received, after all the recent and negative. "Of course!" Ellen replies. "I'm free in the afternoon." Ellen and Karen set a meeting for the next afternoon, and for the first time, there is hope in the office. Ellen immediately starts preparing for meeting and asks her coordinators to get documentation of Greek grades, and Greek volunteering on the island.

Armed with both volunteer hours and GPA's in hand, Ellen heads over to a make or break meeting with Karen Engram.

Questions to consider:

- If you were the administrator in Ellen's position, what would your first three action items be?
- If you were at a higher administrative level, what is your initial gut reaction and first thought when you see NIMU in the news for the alcohol incident?
- Considering the different learning approaches, how would Ellen utilize the behaviorist perspective to create change for her Greek life community or the social constructivist approach?

REFERENCES

Alesandrini, K., & Larson, L. (2002). Teachers Bridge to Constructivism. *The Clearing House: A Journal of Educational Strategies, Issues and Ideas*, *75*(3), 118–121. doi:10.1080/00098650209599249

Bandura, A. (1977). Self-efficacy: Toward a unifying theory of behavioral change. *Psychological Review*, *84*(2), 191–215. doi:10.1037/0033-295X.84.2.191 PMID:847061

Bruner, J. S. (1960). *The Process of education*. Cambridge, MA: Harvard University Press.

Creswell, J., & Poth, C. (2018). *Qualitative Inquiry and Research Design: Choosing Among Five Approaches* (Kindle Edition). Retrieved from Amazon. com

Dewey, J. (1922). *Human nature and conduct*. New York, NY: The Modern Library.

Driscoll, M. P. (2005). *Psychology of learning for instruction*. Boston: Pearson Allyn and Bacon.

Fisher, R., & Ury, W. (2011). *Getting to Yes: Negotiating Agreement Without Giving In*. Penguin Books.

Huitt, W. (2009). *Constructivism. In Educational Psychology Interactive.* Valdosta, GA: Valdosta State University. Retrieved from http://www.edpsycinteractive.org/topics/cognition/construct.html

Kuhn, T. (1962). *The Structure of Scientific Revolutions.* University of Chicago Press.

Merriam, S. B., & Bierema, L. L. (2014). *Adult learning: Linking theory and practice* (Kindle Edition). Retrieved from Amazon.com

Pavlov, I. P. (1910). *The work of the digestive glands.* London: Griffin. Retrieved from https://archive.org/details/workofdigestiveg00pavlrich/page/n17

Piaget, J. (1932). *The moral judgment of the child.* London: Routledge & Kegan Paul.

Popper, K. (1963). *Science: Conjectures and Refutations.* Routledge.

Skinner, B. F. (1938). *The Behavior of Organisms: An Experimental Analysis.* New York: Appleton-Century.

Skinner, B. F. (1948). Superstition' in the pigeon. *Journal of Experimental Psychology, 38*(2), 168–172. doi:10.1037/h0055873 PMID:18913665

Soares, L. (2013). Post-traditional learners and the transformation of postsecondary education: A manifesto for college leaders. *American Council of Education.* Retrieved from http://www.acenet.edu/news-room/Documents/Post-Traditional-Learners.pdf

U.S. Department of Education. (2014). *Ed Performance & Accountability.* Retrieved from https://www2.ed.gov/about/reports/annual/nclbrpts.html

Vygotsky, L. S. (1978). *Mind in society: The development of higher psychological processes.* Harvard University Press.

Watson, J. B., & Rayner, R. (1920). Conditioned emotional reactions. *Journal of Experimental Psychology, 3*(1), 1–14. doi:10.1037/h0069608

Chapter 4
Pedagogy

ABSTRACT

In Chapter 3, the authors consider pedagogy to andragogy. Readers are treated to a brief overview of the pedagogical history and find out when the change from pedagogy to andragogy occurred. Readers will also realize the definition of pedagogy and that pedagogical approaches can be placed on a spectrum from teacher-centered or teacher-directed to learner-centered or learner-directed. The term engagement and, more specifically, student engagement are presented in the chapter. Banking theory will be explored as well as false generosity, active learning, faculty development, and the community of inquiry framework.

INTRODUCTION

Whether you're a first-time instructor, administrator, or a veteran in higher education, the complexity regarding "best practice" can even make a veteran run for the exit. The literature uses multiple terms to refer to best practice. These terms include innovative practice and high impact practice or more commonly referred to as HIP. So, what is HIP? Let's consider earlier literature to help answer this question.

To understand post-traditional leaners' needs, let's turn our eyes to pedagogy, and how the learner has evolved so drastically. "Pedagogy evolved in the monastic schools of Europe between the 7th and 12th centuries. The term is derived from the Greek words *paid*, meaning 'child' and *agogus* meaning 'leader of'" (p. Holmes & Abington-Cooper, 2000, p. 51). In the 1920s

DOI: 10.4018/978-1-7998-0145-0.ch004

Copyright © 2020, IGI Global. Copying or distributing in print or electronic forms without written permission of IGI Global is prohibited.

pedagogical concerns were expressed heavily in research communities. While the majority of research focused on pedagogy, there were some elements of andragogy during this time. Surprisingly to many, the ideas of adult learning and the needs of post-traditional learners have been around since the early 20th century. While Dewey is credited with much of the American ideals on adult learning, Eduard Lindeman's 1926 *The Meaning of Adult Education* provides broad context that is pertinent to this discussion of post-traditional learners. As far back as the early 20th century, a struggle existed between the attempts of nations to standardize learning and still serve the needs of individual learners. Lindeman (1926) writes about efforts to allow free access to education and to standardize education, saying:

We have gone even further and have made certain levels of education compulsory. But the result has been disappointing; we have succeeded merely in formalizing, mechanizing, educational processes. The spirit and meaning of education cannot be enhanced by addition, by the easy method of giving the same dose to more individuals. (p. 4)

Does this sound familiar? Teaching using a pre-designed curriculum or even scripted curriculums, given to all students, regardless of aptitude? The idea of mechanizing is one of the first principles we can glean from traditional literature and pedagogy. For our highlighters: When we seek to design generic programs, or curriculums that don't consider our students diverse needs, we lose our students in the generic motions of the class. If you teach classes and wonder why your students stare at you, barely speak, and are passive, it's not the content; it's you.

For our administrator, smirking, because you don't teach classes and think you've gotten a free pass, this also applies to you. Consider your professional development opportunities, events, guest lectures, committee meetings (We all know how much we love these!), all of these are venues for learning. We're talking about post-traditional learners in this book, but it's important to remember that your professional staff are also lifelong learners, and you directly influence whether they gain knowledge or are inhibited by the method you use to inform them.

From Pedagogy to Andragogy, to now: When did the change happen?
"Since formal education in the United States has focused largely on those between ages 6 and 21, most research before the mid-1960s centered on people in these age groups. Many teachers of adults begin to question the validity of pedagogical assumptions in the early 1960s." (Holmes & Abington-Cooper, 2000, p. 50)

Taking the theoretical to the realistic. One of the best examples of a stark divide between learners left behind or completely supported is the difference in support of those considered "gifted".

Gifted programs. For the uninitiated, there have been many attempts to provide high aptitude students a more challenging curriculum to keep them engaged through their K-12 experience. The Elementary and Secondary Act (ESEA) provides a definition of gifted programs which is "students, children, or youth who give evidence of high achievement capability in areas such as intellectual, creative, artistic, or leadership capacity, or in specific academic fields, and who need services and activities not ordinarily provided by the school in order to fully develop those capabilities" (www.nagc.org). To this end, schools sought to create new curriculum to better support the students. However, after meeting with many students, who were a part of these gifted programs, one of the authors found the programs consisted largely of extra homework. (**Note:** This wasn't every single school, but the majority lack substance in the school's gifted program.) Students cited reasons such as lack of funds, lack of time, or lack of teacher preparation as to why they received so little support. These factors may be a result of variations in state laws, local policies, and district funding (www.nagc.org).

Math and Science Academies. Math and Science Academies, such as TAMS (Texas Academy of Mathematics and Science) or KAMS (Kansas Academy of Mathematics and Science) are state-initiated programs that emphasizes high aptitude students. While not solely focused on gifted students, many of the students recruited come from gifted student pools. Speaking directly from one of the author's experiences working with KAMS, the funding between gifted programs and KAMS is very different. As a program with a direct line in the state budget, KAMS is well funded, providing students the opportunity to come for their junior and senior year of high school to a higher education institution. Their books, tuition, and fees are paid for in this program. KAMS has a dedicated staff consisting of recruiters, directors, counselors, and a strong relationship with the university. Students have an academic advisor assist with classes, in-house tutoring, as well as professors taking time from their regular duties to share their pathway to becoming professors. Students graduate with over 45 credit hours that could transfer to other institutions.

Takeaways. It's easy to see the difference in these two programs. One has a dedicated budget line, with dedicated staff, and a supportive environment for students. The other is an additional job responsibility given to an already overburdened group. This brings up several points.

1) There are a lot of great ideas out there, but if not engaged with the correct resources (time, funding, and preparation), there is a good chance they will fail.

2) For instructors: Age is nowhere near the factor that you may believe it to be. For those teaching undergraduate students who have lowered their expectation because of past students or preconceived notions of what an undergraduate student may be, erase those notions and expectations. While age may have some bearing on student's maturity in dealing with sensitive issues, students will rise to the challenge, and you should feel confident in developing a plan that engages students on multiple levels. (If you're not too sure where to start, take a look at Bloom's Taxonomy, as well as Fink's integrated teaching approach. We'll cover more of this in the instructor chapter).

3) For administrators: There's no sense in starting an initiative if you can't secure the resources needed for it. While there are certainly students who can benefit from changes, overburdening staff to feel good about doing something only exacerbates the problem, causing higher attrition rates when the burden becomes too much to bear. Consider grants, working with the university to dedicate a member to the initiative, and making sure the initiative fits the mission of the institution.

Teaching Methods

Henson (1980) informs us that concepts and uses of the term teaching method are numerous and confusing. Specifically, Henson referred to the terms teaching methods, teaching strategies, and teaching techniques. If this doesn't confuse you, let's add in other terms you may find confusing including pedagogy, pedagogical approaches, pedagogical content knowledge, teacher-centered, teacher-directed, student-centered, student-directed, and didactic practices. Hall, Murphy, and Soler (2008) refer to pedagogy as the "interactions between teachers, students, and the learning environment and the learning tasks" (p. 35). Included in this definition are the relationships between teachers and students and the instructional strategies used in the classroom. Even the term learning can be confusing. For purposes of this text, learning is defined as a process that leads to change, occurring as a result of experience and increasing the potential for improved performance and future learning (Ambrose, et al., 2010). <u>Let us be clear: All of this is jargon</u>. Regardless of the method or approach, using the knowledge presented in the subsequent chapters will help you to better understand the population you're working with, as well as appropriate ways to engage your learners.

Passivity and the Post-Traditional Learner

Now that we have some understanding of where our teaching methods came from, it's important to note how they still affect us today. According to Murphy (2008), pedagogical approaches can be placed on a spectrum from teacher-centered or teacher-directed to learner-centered or learner-directed. "Teacher-directed learning has its roots in Calvinism, and the belief that wisdom is evil, and that adults should direct, control, and ultimately limit children's learning to keep them innocent" (Conner, 2007, para. 4).

Let's stop here for a moment. The basis for our current teaching is designed to limit a child's learning. Now, surely this doesn't mean we purposely withhold information from our learners in higher education…right? Unfortunately, this still holds true in higher education. This belief permeated past generations of learners and still greatly influences the teaching approaches used in many higher education institutions today.

For our highlighters: In a study of 709 STEM courses taught by 548 individual faculty members, Stains et al. (2018) reported that didactic practices still existed in undergraduate STEM curriculums even though these practices had limited impact.

Indeed, a visit to colleges and universities across the United States wound find it hard pressed to NOT find lecture halls. This type of teaching environment is designed for the teacher to be the central focus at the front of the room. The teacher then delivers information to a large number of students sitting in tiered and often permanent seating.

In this type of classroom environment, the primary role of students is to be receptors of information. The English philosopher and physician, John Locke (1632-1704) called this tabula rasa; a Latin term for "scraped tablet"

> Didactic:
> - designed or intended to teach
> - intended to convey instruction and information as well as pleasure and entertainment
> - making moral observations
> "Didactic now sometimes has negative connotations, too, however. Something didactic is often overburdened with instruction to the point of being dull. Or it might be pompously instructive or moralistic" (Merriam-Webster, 2019, p. 1).

where the mind is viewed as a blank slate (https://www.britannica.com/topic/tabula-rasa). In this directed-teacher pedagogic model, teachers assume the responsibility for what is learned, how it's learned, and when something will be learned (Connor, 2007). This idea of students as blank slates, or empty vessels mirrors many of the things that Freire (2000), espouses in his writings, and is something that permeates higher education to this day. Let's break this down further, to really encapsulate what a disservice we do to ourselves and our students.

Higher Education and Oppression

Throughout this book we will journey down several rabbit holes to gain a more holistic view of the post-traditional. One of those rabbit holes deals with the traditions that rooted themselves in higher education, based off of privilege, as well as a patriarchal society. We won't get into all of the logistics, but it's important for us to analyze how these traditions have seeped into our modern-day teaching, as well as the assumptions we use for our learners. Paulo Freire has been at the forefront of progressive moments working against oppression, which includes the post-traditional learner. The following quote is from his book, *Pedagogy of the Oppressed*, and brings about a very subtle, yet truthful statement about learners in the United States higher education system:

Any situation in which "A" objectively exploits "B" or hinder their pursuit of self-affirmation as a responsible person is one of oppression. Such a situation in itself constitutes violence, even when sweetened with false generosity, because it interferes with the individual's ontological and historical vocation to be more fully human. (Freire 2000, p. 55)

In short, Freire (2000) is arguing that regardless of the way you work with someone, if they (or you) are purposely finding ways to deny you opportunities to become more human, this denial is a form of oppression. So what does this mean? How do we quantify a situation in which a learner is exploited?

To understand both this quote and its meaning for higher education, we'll explore the connection between this statement and current U.S. higher education, followed by examples of false generosity higher education has exhibited toward students.

Banking Theory

While higher education espouses ideals of being student-centered, that is not always the case. Freire (2000) describes the idea of Banking theory in his book, and, while written over forty years ago, higher education still has specific fields that use Banking theory. One of the most straightforward examples are classes that are full lecture-based and are under the assumption that students know next to nothing. In many general education courses and to deal with rising costs, students are packed into classrooms like sardines and provided a single teacher for 80+ students. Instead of finding ways to provide critical thinking assignments and engage students in becoming more fully human, professors will instead ascribe to Banking theory, as it is a simple method with which to manage (not teach) all of those students. By sitting in front of a classroom using presentation slides and assuming students know nothing about the content, this is an example of the professor using Banking theory. The professor retains all power and this type of classroom environment forces students to be passive. Teaching using Banking theory, in turn, denies students the opportunity to become more human, and pushes them to be a passive observer in their own life, fulfilling the requirement of false generosity through denying self-affirmation.

False Generosity (need more)

To better understand the idea of false generosity, we need to dig deeper into the idea of becoming fully human. For someone who is oppressed to become more fully human, Freire (2000), argues there are two stages that need to occur to liberate someone from their oppression. Stage one surrounds someone who is oppressed. As someone who is oppressed starts to understand the nature of the oppression that it is currently happening to them, they identify and can make an active commitment to transform the situation. By working through this first stage, the oppressed can identify the issues and nature surrounding oppression, taking concrete steps to end oppression. The second stage occurs after the oppression ends. While the oppression has ended, the ideals of wanting to be fully human are still there. As such, the idea of wanting to be fully human is no longer just the oppressed ideals, but the oppressors also believing in these ideals. Freire (2000) describes this as permanent liberation for all parties involved in the pedagogy of the oppressed. For our highlighters: When we consider our post-traditional learners as empty vessels waiting to be filled, as much as we believe we are liberators in higher education, our purposeful use of certain teaching methods will serve to oppress rather than support our students' learning.

On the surface, this concept may seem irrational, but, consider, your own time as a student, or, as an instructor, the person you would consider the "worst instructor you've ever had in your life". Sadly, most of us have had at least one terrible instructor. The experience may have been the instructor's lack of content familiarity, lack of teaching strategy, use of a monotone voice, and/or a mismatch between the content that was covered and what was assessed. All of these items start adding up. When an instructor doesn't take the time to fully prepare for and understand their learners' experiences, they end up interrupting the students' learning. Students, who see learning as an essential tool for life, are now being robbed of that experience, and thus, the argument could be made that the professor is oppressing that student. If an administrator decides to save money by paying graduate assistants or student workers less money, there is a potential for oppression. Now, this argument needs some common sense. We understand there are many factors that influence institutions' budgets. The point we are trying to make is to consider the gravity of making decisions by placing learners at the forefront of these decisions. Often, the decisions that may seem arbitrary to you, may, in fact, matter a great deal for learners. It is a helpful practice to conduct comprehensive research before making major changes that could impact your learners.

Student learning is the responsibility of both students and institutions (Axelson & Flick, 2010). According to Middlecamp (2005), institutions should provide environments that facilitate learning while students put forth effort to develop their own knowledge and skills.

Higher Education Institution Inequality Mindsets

Malcom-Piqueux and Bensimon (2017) bring up the idea that inequity is often seen as "…an unfortunate, but unavoidable, phenomenon, whose fault lies with students, their families, and communities" (p. 2). We would argue this is the first major problem higher education institutions have. Often time, we work with faculty, administrators, or staff that maintain practices they've used forever. We're sure you've heard or been told but *this is how we've always done it.*

Learning From K-12 and Teacher Education

One of your authors is a former K-12 teacher. Her teacher education training and classroom experiences proved to be an asset to her higher education teaching. As stated by Ambrose, Bridges, DiPietro, Lovett and Norma (2010), "…there are recurring themes among the strategies, such as collecting data about students, modeling expert practice, scaffolding complex tasks, and being explicit about objectives and expectations" (p. 217). The teacher education training that she most frequently called upon included, but were not limited to, the topics of classroom management, lesson objectives, utilizing different types of classroom assessments, providing prompt and specific feedback, and using multiple instructional strategies for content delivery. Let's look at each of the topics areas separately to see how the areas can be applied to instructing higher education learners:

Classroom Management

At the K-12 level, you may recall your teachers telling you to follow the rules. Perhaps the rules were posted on the classroom walls or doors as a constant reminder of what to do. While one would, hopefully, tell post-traditional students to "follow the rules", all learners need to know what to expect from you, the teacher; what you, the teacher, need to expect from them; and what the learners should expect from each other. Dr. Harry Wong, an award-winning K-12 teacher, has published several books on the topic of classroom management. His books are written from a K-12 audience perspective and one of your authors adapted his classroom management techniques for teaching in the higher education classroom. Here's one illustration of classroom management that shows K-12 rule language adapted for post-traditional students.

> **Classroom management**
> <u>K-12 Classroom Rules</u>
> Keep your hands and feet to yourself
> Wait your turn to talk
> Listen to your peers
> Food and drinks only at snack time
> Keep your desk and area clean
> <u>Higher Education (Class) Expectations</u>
> Yourself...
> Come prepared for class
> Clean up any waste before leaving the room
> Use technology devices for class purposes or emergencies
> Each Other...
> Listen to others before speaking
> Instructor...
> Respond to questions within three days of receipt
> Assessments will be graded no later than one week after the original due date

Developing Lesson Objectives

What are lesson objectives and why are they needed at the higher education level? In 1956, Dr, Benjamin Bloom proposed a classification of different objectives and skills for educators to set for their students (learning objectives). The objectives and skills were part of what Bloom referred to as learning for mastery (Bloom, 1968), and later mastery learning (Bloom, 1971). In any teaching lesson, a goal should be to scaffold students' learning to reach a learning outcome. "...Being explicit about one's learning objectives and grading criteria helps students see the component parts of a complex task and thus allows them to target their practice and move toward mastery" (Ambrose, et al., 2010, p. 218). The learning process may take one day or several weeks to finally reach or master an outcome. According to Marzano (2007), "everything being equal, a teacher who designs and organizes academic tasks well will produce better student learning than a teacher who does not" (p. 175). It is the faculty member's responsibility then to plan the learning by preparing lesson objectives for each class period. The objectives may be written in the format - by the end of the lesson, students will...then a verb is used to state one or more of the three main domains of learning which are categorized into cognitive, affective, and psychomotor domains. The lesson objectives should also be communicated to the students and referred to throughout the instruction. To ensure learners have achieved the objective, the selected assessment must align with the lesson objectives.

Utilizing Different Types of Classroom Assessments

There are many ways to assess students' learning in classes. Assessment can be conducted formally and informally. We should also consider learner assessment by differentiating if we are teaching to or for learning. Stiggins (2007) asks us to contemplate moving from a reliance on assessments that verify learning to assessment for learning, that is, assessments that support learning. While not exhaustive, typical classroom assessments include selected-response measures, constructed-response measures, and performance measures. Selected-response types of assessments are represented by multiple-choice, true-false, and matching types of questions. Constructed-response types of assessments includes short answer and essay types of questions. Performance measures, as indicated by the name, assess authentic activities. A well-developed rubric is an excellent method to assess authentic activities.

Goubeaud and Yan (2004) conducted a study that examined teacher educators' instructional practices compared to other education faculty and higher education faculty based on a nationally representative sample of higher education faculty. The sample derived from the National Study of Postsecondary Faculty (NSOPF-93). The authors found that "teacher educators' teaching methods, assessments, and grading practices were significantly different than the education faculty and faculty outside the area of education…" (Goubeaud & Yan, 2004, p. 7). Teacher educators used fewer lectures and more discussion than other education faculty and faculty outside of education. While similar in their use of multiple-choice and short-answer exams, teacher educators used more essay exams, term or research papers, and student evaluations of other students' work. Goubeaud and Yan (2004) concluded that teacher educators were more likely to use performance-based assessments.

Prompt and Specific Feedback

We've all been students in some form or another. As a student, did you ever experience a situation where you completed an assignment, only to wait weeks for a grade? Let's assume that you achieved a grade of C, which is not a bad grade, but it's also not a grade of B or an A. What led the instructor to the grade of C and not a higher (or lower) grade? Knowing what led to the grade helps the learner know what to improve upon for the next related assignment. Let's assume the next related assignment was due before you received the specific feedback on the assignment where you achieved the grade of C. Unless you have psychic powers, there's no way for you to reflect upon the C assignment feedback to improve your grade on the next assignment. Prompt and specific feedback also helps the instructor. After all, the majority of instructors want their students to do well in class. The higher students' achievement, the less correction is needed on students' assessments. Students meeting the assignment's expectations also signals that your students are ready to move on to learn new content.

Using Multiple Instructional Strategies for Content Delivery

In Goubeaud and Yan's (2004) study, they found that teacher educators used fewer lectures and more discussion than other education faculty and faculty outside of education. Why is this important? Ambrose, et al. (2010) stated that teaching requires knowing when various teaching strategies and instructional approaches are applicable. These authors used an example of learning objectives and deciding if the objectives would best be met by group work, case studies or multiple-choice tests.

So which strategy works? Is there one model of effective teaching? Marzano (2007) states "in short, research will never be able to identify instructional strategies that work with every student in every class. The best research can do is tell which strategies have a good chance (i.e., high probability) of working well with students" (p. 5). While the authors generally agree with Marzano, there's also research that indicates problem-based learning (PBL) may be advantageous for adult learners. More about PBL will be considered later in this chapter. Although Marzano indicates little likelihood that research will identify instructional strategies that work with every student in every class, he does advocate for student engagement.

Active Learning

Historically, there have been hints of active learning as far back as a hundred years. Recently, Freeman et al. (2014) has become one of the most heavily cited and recent pieces of literature regarding active learning. One takeaway in this study is that students in a traditional learning environment such as lecture "…were 1.5 times more likely to fail than were students in classes with active learning" (Freeman et al., 2014, p. 1).

> Fun fact: The phrase 'student engagement' is referred to as "how involved or interested students appear to be in their learning and how connected they are to their classes, their institutions, and each other" (Axelson & Flick, 2010, p. 38).

> Middlecamp (2005) offered three reasons for engagement: to know and connect with students, to have students engage with the teacher, and as an intellectual challenge. The National Survey of Student Engagement (NSSE, 2003) describes engagement as involvement in rich educational opportunities, active and collaborative learning, participation in challenging academic activities, and reinforced by learning communities.

Some strategies that support student engagement, according to Marzano (2007), are games. "Games stimulate attention because they involve missing information" (p. 103). Other approaches to engage students include physical movement, appropriate pacing, intensity and enthusiasm for the content, and opportunities for students to talk to each other (Marzano, 2007). Rosenshine (2012) presented ten research-based strategies derived from research in cognitive science, master teachers, and cognitive supports. He explains that cognitive supports refer to effective instructional procedures which derive from the field of cognitive science. Rosenshine (2012) concluded there are at least ten effective strategies. They include the following:

Begin a lesson with a short review of previous learning. Present new material in small steps with student practice after each step. Ask a large number of questions and check the responses of all students. Provide models. Guide student practice. Check for student understanding. Obtain a high success rate. Provide scaffolds for difficult tasks. Require and monitor independent practice. Engage students in weekly and monthly review. (p. 12)

We said we'd get to the PBL strategy later in the chapter. We've arrived. PBL or problem-based learning can be traced to John Dewey and the Progressive philosophy that teachers should teach by appealing to students' natural instincts to investigate and create (Delisle, 1997). PBL is defined as "a teaching method in which students gain knowledge and skills by working for an extended period of time to investigate and respond to an authentic, engaging, and complex question, problem, or challenge" (https://www.pblworks.org/what-is-pbl, para

---

Recap area:
- Active learning helps learners to better comprehend material (Freeman et al., 2014).
- Active and collaborative learning are nationally recognized, and endorsed for the gains seen in students (NSSE, 2003).
- Students are more engaged in content and will take more risks when there is an authentic conversation (Auger, 2003).
- Creating an interactive environment supports learner success (Gaytan and McEwen, 2007).
- Developing communities emphasizing learning help students to development more confidence, competence, and meaning from activities (Kuh et al., 2008).

---

3). According to Hilarius, Herwati, and Newcomb (2019), implementing the PBL model through a practicum supported with authentic assessment was more effective as compared to the PBL model and conventional learning. The Gold Standard Project Based Learning by PBL Works is licensed under CC BY-NC-ND 4.0 and includes seven design elements of PBL. The design elements are a challenging problem or question, sustained inquiry, authenticity, student voice and choice, reflection, critique and revision, and public product.

Higher Education Faculty Development Programs

The information in this chapter, thus far, informed us about pedagogy and pedagogical changes. While helpful, knowing the information will NOT change teachers' practices but comprehensive and sustainable faculty development programs can. Research into faculty development is a more recent development that includes studies on faculty workloads, courses, student generated hours, and specific teaching strategies (Major & Palmer, 2006). Faculty development began to emerge in higher education in the United States in the late 1950s and 1960s (Gillespie & Robertson, 2010). As cited in Gillespie and Robertson (2010), "Sorcinelli, et al. (2006) categorized the evolution of faculty development into four ages (scholar, teacher, developer, and learner) and one new one (the age of the networker)" (p. 5). In 2006, Sorcinelli, Austin, Eddy and Beach reported five priorities faculty developers saw as challenges for faculty in higher education. They stated that one priority was the challenge to balance the increasingly complex and demanding faculty roles. Another priority was assessment of teaching and student learning especially in the context of increasingly diverse students. Realizing the impact of technology was third priority. A fourth priority was to address the needs of part-time faculty. Finally, a fifth priority was to consider interdisciplinary leadership as an area of development for chairs and institutions.

Learning as We Go

One of your authors is experiencing a great need for faculty development and has begun steps to develop a comprehensive and sustainable faculty (and staff) development program. Thankfully, an institution's Title III grant allowed the hire of a short-term consultant to help facilitate the creation of a comprehensive and sustainable faculty and staff development program. As of the writing of this book, the faculty and staff development program has not been completed. However, working collaboratively with key stakeholders, the program's framework includes four goals and ten key performance indicators (KPI) with identified tasks for each KPI. The four major goals are 1) to create and implement a multi-faceted delivery system, 2) increase opportunities to develop better communication to improve relationships, 3) increase and maintain the relevance of the professional development program and 4) increase the integrated use of technology. To create and implement a multi-faceted delivery system, consideration needs to be given to the type of delivery system. One option is centripetally, that is, services provided by asking faculty and staff to come to a physical or electronic location. The other option is to deliver services, centrifugally, which is to go where the faculty and staff are located or sending out electronic information. Both types of delivery systems will be needed. In terms of the second and third goals, college and institutional restraints dictated the program would need to be created, organically, and there would be not be a central person, like a director, overseeing the faculty and staff development program. When considering increasing the integrated use of technology, goal number four, Kuhlenschmidt (2010), states there are four tasks to examine regarding the effective use of technology for faculty development:

The first task is understanding faculty members' attitudes toward technology. The second is choosing appropriate technology. The third is using knowledge of clients and objectives to help faculty members integrate technology teaching. The fourth is implementing appropriate technology for the various programs and goals....(p. 259)

The next phase of creating the professional development program will be the most time-consuming part. It is the implementation phase which relies somewhat on market research. Examples of research include surveys, event evaluations, focus groups, advisory committees, individual interviews, and observations (Zakrajsek, 2010). In the author's situation, some market research exists, but more must be gathered to truly create a meaningful and sustained faculty and staff professional development program.

CHAPTER FOUR SUMMARY

Chapter four shared Henson's (1980) thoughts on concepts and terms, such as teaching methods, that can be confusing to many people. Pedagogy is another overused term. Understanding the nature of these terms, helps us appreciate the limitations of some current teaching practices. Additionally, knowledge of Banking theory allows us to relate learning opportunities that are denied to students. This chapter also provided lessons learned from K-12 and teacher education for replication in higher education classes. Finally, the chapter offered "learning on the go" regarding faculty development programs, which are one way to support teachers' instructional practices.

REFERENCES

Ambrose, S. A., Bridges, M. W., DiPietro, M., Lovett, M. C., & Norman, M. K. (2010). *How learning works: 7 research-based principles for smart teaching*. San Francisco, CA: Jossey-Bass.

Auger, T. (2003, May). Student-centered reading: A review of the research on literature circles. *EPS Update Newsletter*. Retrieved from https://eps. schoolspecialty.com/EPS/media/Site-Resources/Downloads/articles/ Literature_Circles.pdf

Axelson, R. D., & Flick, A. (2010). Defining student engagement. *Change: The Magazine of Higher Learning*, *43*(1), 38–43. doi:10.1080/00091383.2 011.533096

Bloom, B. S. (1968). Learning for mastery. *Evaluation Comment*, *1*(2), 1-12.

Bloom, B. S. (1971). Mastery learning. In J. H. Block (Ed.), *Mastery learning: Theory and practice*. New York: Holt, Rinehart & Winston.

Bucks Institute for Education. (n.d.). Retrieved from www.pblworks.org

Connor, M. L. (2007). *Andragogy and pedagogy.* Retrieved March 1, 2007, from http://agelesslearner.com/intros/andragogy.html

Delisle, R. (1997). *How to use problem-based learning in the classroom.* Alexandria, VA: ASCD.

Encyclopedia Brittanica. (2019, February 25). *Tabula rasa philosophy.* Retrieved from https://www.britannica.com/topic/tabula-rasa

Freeman, S., Eddy, S., Mcdonough, M., Smith, M., Nnadozie, O., Jordt, H., & Wenderoth, M. (2014). Active learning increases student performance in science, engineering, and mathematics. *Proceedings of the National Academy of Sciences of the United States of America, 111*(23), 8410–8415. doi:10.1073/pnas.1319030111 PMID:24821756

Freire, P. (2000). *Pedagogy of the oppressed: 30th Anniversary Edition* (Kindle Edition). Retrieved from Amazon.com

Gaytan, J., & McEwen, B. C. (2007). Effective online instructional and assessment strategies. *American Journal of Distance Education, 21*(3), 117–123. doi:10.1080/08923640701341653

Gillespie, K. J., & Robertson, D. L. (2010). A guide to faculty development (2nd ed.). San Francisco, CA: Jossey-Bass.

Goubeaud, K., & Yan, W. (2004). Teacher educators' teaching methods, assessments, and grading: A comparison of higher education faculty's instructional practices. *Teacher Educator, 40*(1), 1–16. doi:10.1080/08878730409555348

Hall, K., Murphy, P., & Soler, J. (2008). *Pedagogy and practice: Culture and identities.* Los Angeles, CA: SAGE.

Henson, K. T. (1980). Teaching Methods: Designs for Learning. *Theory into Practice, 19*(1), 2–5. doi:10.1080/00405848009542864

Hilarius, J. D., Herawati, S. H., & Newcomb, P. (2019). Enhancing different ethnicity science process skills: Problem-based learning through practicum and authentic assessment. *International Journal of Instruction, 12*(1), 1207–1222. doi:10.29333/iji.2019.12177a

Holmes, G., & Abington-Cooper, M. (2000). Pedagogy vs. Andragogy: A false Dichotomy. *The Journal of Technology Studies, 26*(2), 50–55. doi:10.21061/jots.v26i2.a.8

Kuh, G. D., Cruce, T. M., Shoup, R., Kinzie, J., & Gonyea, R. M. (2008). Unmasking the effects of student engagement on first-year college grades and persistence. *The Journal of Higher Education*, 79(5), 540–563. doi:10.1080/00221546.2008.11772116

Kuhlenschmidt, S. (2010). Issues in technology and faculty development. In K. J. Gillespie & L. Robertson (Eds.), *A Guide to Faculty Development* (2nd ed.; pp. 259–274). San Francisco, CA: Jossey-Bass.

Lindeman, E. (1926). The meaning of adult education. New Republic Inc.

Major, C. H., & Palmer, B. (2006). Reshaping Teaching and Learning: The Transformation of Faculty Pedagogical Content Knowledge. *Higher Education*, 51(4), 619–647. doi:10.100710734-004-1391-2

Malcom-Piqueux & Bensimon. (2017). Taking Equity-Minded Action to Close Equity Gaps. *peerReview, 19*(2).

Martin, E., Prosser, M., Trigwell, K., Ramsden, P., & Benjamin, J. (2000). What university teachers teach and how they teach it. *Instructional Science*, 28(5), 387–412. doi:10.1023/A:1026559912774

Marzano, R. J. (2007). *The art and science of teaching: A comprehensive framework for effective instruction*. Alexandria, VA: ASCD.

Merriam-Webster. (2019). *Didactic*. Retrieved from https://www.merriam-webster.com/dictionary/didactic

Middlecamp, C. H. (2005). The art of engagement. *Peer Review: Emerging Trends and Key Debates in Undergraduate Education*, 7(2), 17–20.

Murphy, P. (2008). Defining pedagogy. In K. Hall, P. Murphy, & J. Soler (Eds.), *Pedagogy and practice: Culture and identities* (pp. 28–39). London: Sage Publications.

National Association for Gifted Children. (n.d.). Retrieved from https://www.nagc.org/resources-publications/resources/frequently-asked-questions-about-gifted-education

National Survey of Student Engagement. (2003). *National survey of student engagement 2003*. Retrieved from http://nsse.indiana.edu/2003_annual_report/pdf /NSSE_2003_Annual_Report.pdf

Rosenshine, B. (2012, Spring). Research-based strategies that all teachers should know. American Educator, 12-19, 39.

Sorcinelli, M. D., Austin, A. E., Eddy, P. L., & Beach, A. L. (2006). *Creating the future of faculty development: Learning from the past, understanding the present.* Boston, MA: Anker.

Stiggins, R. (2007). Assessment through the student's eyes. *Educating the Whole Child, 64*(8), 22–26.

Zakrajsek, T. D. (2010). Important skills and knowledge. In A guide to faculty development (2nd ed.; pp. 83-98). San Francisco, CA: Jossey-Bass.

Chapter 5

For Administrators:
Changing High Impact Practices to Reflect All Learners

ABSTRACT

As administrators, you have a unique role in the support of post-traditional learners. As your capacity may be in either student or academic affairs, the authors will attempt to highlight each of the areas in a way that can be useful to either role. Self-concept is a building block that good administrators acknowledge and account for when developing policies. Learners are major stakeholders at your institution and will develop internal coalitions with faculty and professional staff if their ability to pursue their educational goals is interrupted. If policies are stifling, learners may decide not to persist, which directly affects the health of the institution.

INTRODUCTION

You've made it through most of the book, great job! (Or, maybe you skipped to the tips, either way, you're here.) We'll outline several important concepts in this chapter and present some of the most important changes that could affect post-traditional learners in our higher education institutions

DOI: 10.4018/978-1-7998-0145-0.ch005

Copyright © 2020, IGI Global. Copying or distributing in print or electronic forms without written permission of IGI Global is prohibited.

Simple Tips for Curriculum Success

In the earlier chapters, one of the biggest changes we've touched upon is how much the curriculum matters. While external accrediting bodies and internal program reviews require institutions to follow specific guidelines, other factors have influenced higher education curricula. Including curriculum, one of the major factors, is developmental education.

Imagine this scenario - A post-traditional learner did not do well in high school or on a college entrance exam like the ACT or SAT. As a result, the learner landed in a lower level or remedial math course at the institution. The remedial course is required for the learner to pass to be able to enroll in a 100-level math class required to graduate. The learner completes this class in the first semester, but, because of the learner's lack of math knowledge and skills, the learner needs to take an additional remedial class to be able to enroll in the required 100-level class. The learner takes the second remedial class in the following semester. The learner finds out his job is transferring him to another area. After a full year of college, the learner has still not enrolled in the 100-level math course that is required for graduation. The learner finds a new institution but is told the remedial courses aren't considered general education courses and will not transfer. Like the previous institution, the new institution requires specific high school grades and college entrance exam scores which the learner does not have. The cycle then repeats with the learner forced to take the new institution's remedial classes.

If you were this student, what would you do? Personally, we would probably throw our hands up and not think too fondly of the first institution nor of the time lost because the two classes did not transfer. The saddest part? This scenario is far more common then we and we're sure you, too, would like. It is with this example that we now examine developmental education.

Developmental Education

Developmental education is found at many higher education institutions. According to the Center for the Analysis of Postsecondary Readiness, the majority of students at community colleges and a fairly large percentage of students at four-year colleges take developmental education courses (Development, n.d.). Additionally, *findings from a nationally representative study suggest that students who complete their developmental courses are more likely than partial completers or noncompleters to stay in college and earn a bachelor's degree—but the results vary depending on students' level of academic preparation. Dev ed helps weakly prepared students on several indicators. But moderately or strongly prepared community college students who complete some of their developmental courses are worse off than similar students who take no remedial courses in terms of college-level credits earned, transfer to a four-year college, and bachelor's degree attainment. Other studies have found little or no positive effect from enrolling in developmental courses.* (Development, n.d., *para. 4).*

For some students, completing developmental education courses becomes a barrier to a learner earning the degree, costing both time and money. However, there is an alternative to the current structure of remedial classes. It is one idea we believe could be incredibly beneficial for post-traditional learners.

As mentioned earlier in this chapter, it is highly likely that post-traditional learners will be required to complete some developmental education courses. We know from Tinto (2016) that understanding the curriculum is important for our learners, thus we need to be transparent in our desires for learner success, as well as intentional in our curriculum design.

Redesigning Remedial Pathways

One way to better serve your post-traditional learners is to redesign remedial pathways. Currently, "research indicates traditional developmental course-taking can increase students' time to degree attainment and decrease their likelihood of completion" (Schak et al, 2017, p. 7). Typically, remedial classes take the form of non-transferable courses that may hold back learners on their paths to success. By redesigning a required general education class, this would allow the credits to count and better serve the learner. Let's use an example of an Introduction to College Algebra course. Imagine this class is required for undergraduate degree-seekers and is most often offered as a three-credit hour course. However, the pass rate for this class is only around 60%. For the learners you know will struggle, the Introduction to College Algebra course becomes an immense bottleneck for learners working their way to complete their degrees. This bottleneck is exacerbated by remedial classes that take the entire semester. One way to can combat this is by compressing or mainstreaming developmental education (Schak et al, 2017). The bottleneck is not in classes for their chosen major; it is this singular class. By creating a course that is quicker, and more intensive, you can help to mitigate some of the time issues a learner faces, as well as potential cost.

This includes another concept known as "co-requisite pathways" (Schak et al, 2017, p. 13). Co-requisite pathways add a concurrent academic support class, which learners take as a supplemental course. Schak et al. (2017) explains that not only does this lower a student's time to complete their degree, it also helps reduce the cost associated with remedial classes. Some some studies show a boost in pass rates up 28% for introductory college-writing (p. 13). By compressing or mainstreaming your developmental courses, as well as introducing co-requisite pathways, you can keep your learners on track, help them save money, and provide an overall boost to your institutions success rate with developmental courses.

Offering Prior Learning Credit

While it is becoming a staple at many institutions, a second options is to offer prior learning credit. This can be accomplished by gathering a committee and benchmarking requirements against some of the more progressive institutions in your region. A support for the benchmarking is to reach out to your professional associations to learn what insights can be offered in creating the process. An area to pay particular attention to includes policies regarding categories or types of prior learning. For example, one category of prior learning is students earning credit for work experiences. Another category of prior learning is awarding credit to learners who have completed certification in an area applicable to their field of study. Regardless of the category of prior learning experience, it is important to consider how external accreditation will view these types of learning experiences. To help make a case for the prior learning credit with external accrediting bodies, a template is recommended. Suggested template items include identifying educational learning objectives and explaining how the activities meet the required number credit hours. The following are a sampling of activities to consider: the number of and approximate time to complete readings, discussions, presentations, and projects. To stay in compliance, make sure you're interacting with other institutions that have the same accreditation.

Consistent, Expedited Courses

For many post-traditional learners, they may only be able to take one or two classes at a time. But, doing so, does not mean these learners need to fall behind. You can design a consistent, course schedule that is expedited for your post-traditional learners. Courses can be offered in one-, four-, or eight-week time periods. By offering classes in such a manner, you can effectively allow your learners to stay on track and reach graduation at a faster rate. At one of the author's institutions, learners can take two courses per each eight-week term. The courses are offered on-campus in the evening and/or online. Enrolling in two courses is considered full-time which is required if students are using full-time financial aid. If a learner is enrolled in two courses each eight-week period and there are five eight-week periods throughout the calendar year, a student could theoretically complete a 123-credit hour bachelor's degree in four years. The learner would need to enroll in one term for nine credit hours or opt to complete a one-week intensive term. This example assumed no transfer or prior learning credit had been earned. However, many post-traditional students will come to an institution with some type of earned credit. In these cases, it will take less than four years for learners with existing credits. By creating a consistent rotation of course offerings, learners, choosing to stop out for a term, won't feel they're missing too much time, will be more likely to persist, and this creates a more flexible environment for the learner.

Moving on from some of our general tips for success, we turn back to ways to apply theory to better serve your post-traditional learners. As administrators, you have a unique role in the support of post-traditional learners. Since your role may be either academic or student affairs, we will highlight each of the following areas to illustrate how these concepts can be useful to either role.

Self-Concept

Self-concept is a building block that good administrators acknowledge, and account for when developing policies. Learners are major stakeholders at your institution. They will develop internal coalitions with faculty and professional staff if their ability to pursue their educational goals is interrupted. If policies are stifling, learners may decide not to persist, which directly affects the health of the institution.

Learner self-concept is important to not only the instructor but also to you. Many of the learners you meet may be in other roles such as contributing locally in the community or perhaps even on campus in some capacity. At a larger institution you may not know everyone in academic or student affairs, but more than likely the learners either have a stake in the institution, or, they will become a stakeholder in some capacity, even if that capacity is solely as learners. Self-concept is important because of the notions of internal coalitions and policy creation.

Internal Coalitions and Mentorship

The success of your institutions hinders on your stakeholders, including your instructors, professionals, and learner populations. In order to successfully navigate some of the complexities of being a champion for your institution as well as your learners, we'll use the following example to illustrate the importance of navigating internal coalitions:

A new president has just joined the institution. The previous president was well respected, but had been at the institution for well over fifteen years. As a result, there was a general understanding of the status quo, and both academic and student affairs knew where they were ranked at the institution. With the changing of the guard, the new president is in a position to make waves, even if this president did nothing. As the new president gears up to lead, several projects stemming from the president's vision are enacted. The change in leadership, coupled with the realization there will be changes, has led to several faculty retiring. The institutional migration leaves the new president with staffing challenges along with the challenge of helping the stakeholders understand the president's leadership style.

Does this example sound familiar? Did you experience a similar issue when you became an administrator? Often, many administrators enter a new role as director, chair, dean, etc., by entering an environment that is neutral at best! While there will be employees who relish the change, more often there are misgivings when someone new arrives. The misgivings are especially true if the new leader moves quickly to make immediate changes. As an administrator, your position requires you to navigate the complexities of these new relationships. This new navigation is exactly the same for incoming post-traditional learners. Consider an incoming post-traditional learner who is older, has experience as a sole earner, is used to a different work environment, and is now a brand new learner starting in the classroom. The dynamic of entering with previous work experience means previous norms don't apply, and thus the learner's initial experience can be equated to your first time in an administrative role. Looking back, what type of actions did you perform to understand the internal coalitions in the institution? Our recommendations are the following:

Make It a Point to Meet With the Learners

- If you are on the academic side, schedule a block of time to meet with learners. This could take the form of a luncheon, an informal walk around to meet learners in dedicated study spaces or welcoming learners as they arrive through the main entrance to the building. Visiting classes at the beginning of a term, whether this is a semester, trimester, quarter or some other configuration, will allow you to get to know your learners much better, and creates a sense of visibility that may be enough to help solidify a learner's feelings of belonging at the institution.
- If you are on the student affairs side, lean heavily on the associations on campus. These could be student government, student organizations, or volunteer groups. Dedicate an hour of your time per week to meet different groups, especially in the evening. The post-traditional population of learners may be the earner for their families. As a result, they may come later in the day, evening, or on the weekend. While we advocate for some type of work and life balance, it's important to flex your time to meet your learners when they are most available. Many larger universities will have a specific area dedicated to off campus commuters, which constitutes a large amount of the post-traditional learner populations.

Create Opportunities for Community

From the previous chapters that mentioned theory, we know learners need a sense of belonging. As you consider your role on the academic or student affairs side of your institution, keep in mind that you have the opportunity to create community through policy and procedures. This can be done in the following ways:

- On the academic side, you have the opportunity to reach a very specific set of post-traditional learners, namely, those within your specific college or school. If you work with a group that isn't defined, consider the following statements through the lens of your interaction with post-traditional learners. Design at least one activity per semester focused on developing relationships between your post-traditional learners or ask for assistance with designing if your plate is full and attend.
- On the student affairs side, there are several possibilities to better create communities for your post-traditional learners. The first is to identify a space within your institution for post-traditional learners. By designating an area for post-traditional learners, you can center both dialogue and resources in it. If you're working in events, resources include things like childcare and evening activities. The intent is to create a space that says to the post-traditional learner that you belong.

The Role of Experience

Learners need venues to use their previous experience. Hiring well informed instructors that utilize active learning techniques will go a long way towards students' knowledge retention, satisfaction, and soft skill development. Consider funding, heading or designing events that allow students to demonstrate their experience.

- In the academic side, experience plays a valuable role in a learner's educational journey. As an administrator, there are some key areas of changes that you can make to better support your post-traditional learners. Examples of ways to support these learners include new hire training and the implementation of co-curricular events.

New Hire Advertising

As an administrator, you will have at least some influence on the hiring and training process of new hires. With that in mind, there are several ways you can influence the process. First, make sure you add explicit language in your job advertisements regarding the support of post-traditional learners. As this concept is still relatively new to the academic world, your candidates that speak about it will have at least looked up the concept. This can be an easy way to see if your candidates have taken the initiative to research the position and institution for which they applied, while also giving them an understanding of the post-traditional learner population.

- On the academic side, knowledge of post-traditional learners' needs will be especially important for your incoming instructors, as they will have a direct influence on the classroom. Testing their knowledge of active learning, as well as how to work with learners' returning to the classroom will help weed out those who refuse to change their teaching style to accommodate diverse learners, which goes beyond our post-traditional learner population. Other incoming new hire roles that should have knowledge of this population include academic advisors, who need to be aware of the need for flexibility classes, as well as your fellow administrators, as the policies they develop will be the backbone to learner interactions.

- Involve both your adjuncts as well as full-time professors in a one-time training. This can be a short, one hour training covering elements of chapter one of this book. By bringing attention to post-traditional learners' needs, you can help both your new and experienced professors critically engage in the topic, and listen to strategies that some may already be using. As a population, post-traditional learners heavily benefit from adult learning theory teaching methods, (as do most learners), so if you're looking for some go to ideas for working with this population, you can incorporate work from the theoretical frameworks discussed in chapter two, as well as this chapter. Remember, this is about exposing your instructors to a population that is continually growing on campus, and one that will benefit heavily from understanding their needs.

- On the student affairs side, this area touches almost every element of learners' interactions as they pursue their education. Between student services, housing, and events, learners will have a high propensity for interaction with your staff. Thus, however cliché, every incoming hire should have at least a basic knowledge of post-traditional learners. Now, we realize that this may not feasible in your administrative position, so your emphasis should be on any areas that you have the ability to influence before, during and after the hiring process. Areas that could benefit most from this knowledge are student involvement areas, orientation, and advising.

> Note: Professional organizations are a great resource for trainings. If you're hesitant to send your professionals to conferences, integrate their learning into conference or webinar experiences. We know from research that our learners learn better if they teach others, and that continues even after finishing a degree. Have you heard of life-long learning? You can require your staff to give a presentation on concepts they learned from a conference or have them perform research to become content experts. The more you and they know, the better your learners' experience.

- As we look towards co-curriculums and demonstrating the amazing work of student affairs professionals, we need to change and adapt to a new mindset. One of the changes is to reset our focus from being student affairs administrators to a more faculty-oriented mindset. Before you throw out this book out, hear us out. One of the main reasons faculty continue to flourish is an emphasis on professional development. While you may be crying out "I'm in NASPA, NACADA, or NACA!", professional development should also be present on our campuses, and have a continuous presence in meetings. Consider choosing a topic per month for a presentation, and use meeting times to engage in new research in your respective area. This doesn't have to be the entire session, just a dedicated time to continue to professionally develop. You may be amazed at how much professionals want to engage in new research. [As a note, one of your authors is a member and currently on the IV-W board of NASPA and is also a NACA member.]

Readiness to Learn

With our emphasis on the curriculum in higher education, we may miss the critical moment when a learner requires immediate knowledge on a subject, solely because we have assigned it as the following topic.

Your learners aren't contacting you because of a whim. They've already made the decision to pursue higher education when they contact you. Thus, to foster the best experience for the university and the learner, there are several ways to prepare your institution. Your first step should be policy changes.

Policy Changes

Learners coming into higher education have already experienced at least some of what the world outside higher education looks like. In their own lives, most things are now instantly available at their fingertips. The ability to pick and choose whichever type of food, clothing, and educational services they wish. As administrators, we need to be cognizant of this shift. Many consumers would immediately pass by higher education if they could, with outdated or arbitrary policies related to taking classes, extra fees, and the lack of streamlining of services. Our suggestions are as follows.

- On the academic affairs side, the emphasis for your department should be on streamlining both the application process, as well as the services you provide. Long wait times between application submission and review will result in learners choosing to withdraw their application and, most likely, choosing another institution that was timely with confirmation of acceptance. Consider your current in-house processes, how long does it take from start to finish to get an application processed then ultimately reviewed?
- On the student affairs side, policies surrounding learner access to services, as well as the orientation process can make or break learners' experiences. As stated above, there is a stark contrast in the expectations of learners now in higher education compared to thirty years ago. We are viewed in many ways as an investment, and one that learners expect will start to immediately pay dividends. Policies that allow learners to access services in a quick and timely fashion will support both the mission and the learners' desires for a sense of belonging.

CURRICULUM

- On the academic affairs side, we recommend following the tips provided at the beginning of this chapter, including making your developmental education count towards an undergraduate degree, create a consistent schedule for courses, as well as expedited course schedules. One final recommendation is to weave the curriculum directly into tangible skills. During and after completing their degrees, post-traditional learners want to use their knowledge and skills in their work. By being explicit in your curriculum, including course descriptions, as well as recruiting materials, your learners will have a better sense of the value of the education you will offer to them.
- On the student affairs side, one of the newest ways to shine, co-curriculums are the bread and butter to successful post-traditional learner success. Co-curriculums are generally designed around having

learners attend campus events, writing reflections, and are created with different learning objectives. Providing different ways to achieve those objectives (e.g. attending an event, reflecting on an attended conference, etc.) learners have the flexibility to achieve the co-curriculum and receive something tangible. As with academic affairs, creating ways to show employers tangible skills can be a sticking point for student affairs professionals. If you haven't invested in co-curriculums, benchmark with other institutions. Good places to start include developing a leadership co-curriculum and having it placed on a students' academic transcript after they complete it. Post-traditional learners will see the direct relation to potential wage increases, as you provide another opportunity for learners to grow.

Orientation to Learning

For post-traditional learners, learning has shifted from a subject-centered curriculum to one of problem-centered education. Often, there are experiences in a post-traditional learners' life that require more knowledge, and a sense of immediacy in gaining that knowledge.

Previously discussed in the readiness to learn section, post-traditional learners have a sense of immediacy in their education. This leads to a unique challenge for administrators. How do we provide a venue for post-traditional learners that is flexible, yet rigorous? If we were to develop a venue, how would we support our learners to the caliber of or even better than our "go to" face to face courses? The answer has been slowly, yet surely coming to higher education. I'm speaking of hybrid courses and technology for distance learners.

Hybrid Courses

Courses offered in the hybrid format can provide a more conducive schedule for post-traditional learners. Some institutions engage working adults by emphasizing evening and weekend classes. This involves fewer in-person or ground class meetings with the addition of online content to supplement course instruction. For example, a hybrid course may meet as little as three times over the course of fifteen weeks or as much as every other week. By reducing the number of days post-traditional learners need to be on the campus could mean saving on the cost of babysitters or day care, less drive time to and from campus, less gas expense and wear and tear on vehicles, and more time to spend with the family. A prime example of the benefit of a hybrid course is the learner taking advantage of fixed tuition for adjacent states. The learner may be four or more hours away, thus the travel distance is a direct factor in the decision to attend. Many institutions also offer online classes, yet not all learners are successful in online environments. The mix of the face to face presence and the online instruction may help post-traditional learners be more successful. As an administrator, consider creating a trial run of a hybrid course starting with weekend classes. While weekend instruction may not be the preference for some instructors, the goal should be to support your post-traditional learners.

Delivery Courses

Delivery, arriving in thirty minutes, or it's free? Not exactly. If you can't beat them, join them. Institutions are now hosting classes in major learner hubs and at companies, instead of only offering classes at the institutions. Learner cohorts can exist in other locations. Time can be built-in for campus instructors be at the location a few times during the course time period. Another option is to hire one or more designated instructors who live in the area to instruct the courses. In short, these delivery options allow programs to engage a much larger learner population than normal, while still maintaining face to face elements.

Distance Learners and Robots

Technology – there's the good and the bad. In higher education, some people who would argue that technology is eroding the educational landscape, while other people would argue the impact of technology in providing learners with more access to education. Many learners live in areas that are too far away for learners to drive each day or even every other day to class. Our position is technology innovations can better support our learners. One newer technology is telepresence in conjunction with robots to engage learners more effectively in the classroom. While we won't note specific companies in this book, several companies have already created machines that allow learners to remotely engage in classes. Imagine video conferencing software that allows you to see a learners' face and has the ability to turn toward others for group work or discussion. Technology advances allow learners to fully engage in a classroom even when they can't be physically present.

Motivation to Learn

In a previous chapter, we discussed learners' internal and external motivations. *As a reminder, intrinsic motivation is a student's desire to engage in an activity without an external pressure. While some students are motivated, externally, post-traditional learners focus more on internal motivation.*

When considering a learner's motivation, there is a proven way to identify and support your learners need. Ask. Your learners are there for a reason. It could be for a promotion at work. It could be to explore a brand-new career. It could be any number of reasons, but the easiest way to engage your learners is to understand their motivation for being there. As administrators, this can be a challenging notion depending on your role at the institution. You may have little to no face to face contact with your post-traditional learner population but are still indirectly influencing the population through policy. Here are a few recommendations to consider:

- **Buddy Up** – Meeting with a few post-traditional learners can help develop good mentoring opportunities, but it may take more than a small sample size of post-traditional learners to meet the outcome. Instead of tapping into only a few learners that you know, focus on buddying up. When we say "buddy up", we mean find intentional relationships that could lead to more insight into the population on your campus. Many institutions have a post-traditional learner population on campus. Your first step should be to consider forming a relationship with instructors who engage with post-traditional learners. Often, there are post-traditional learners, online, as well as in classes offered during the weekends.
- **Assessment Support -** You could also meet with your co-workers involved in institutional assessment for help to develop a survey to administer to post-traditional leaners. The survey can provide a better overall understanding the campus climate as viewed from the perspectives of post-traditional learners. By collaborating with others at your institution, not only do you find answers, you indirectly provide people with information that makes them more aware of the post-traditional learner population on the campus!

CHAPTER FIVE CONCLUSION

Chapter five provided several tangible ways to use theory, learning frameworks, and knowledge of post-traditional learners to better serve your post-traditional population on campus. Through an intentional re-examination of policy and procedures, institutions can make a lasting change for their learners, as well as potentially increase learner persistence rates. With the current knowledge from this chapter in mind, consider the case study provided below. This case study provides you with an opportunity to consider how you would approach needed changes to support post-traditional learners. After reading the case study, answer the prompts with this chapter's content in mind.

Case Studies for Administrators

Technology Woes

As an administrator, you find your instructors' technology skills are woefully lacking. And students are complaining. They are tired of presentation slides and have a hard time understanding why instructors choose to use DVDs. Surely, teachers can find the resources they need by searching the internet. Besides the students' concerns, maintaining DVD players is not where you want to spend your budget and supporting this older equipment is not fondly viewed by the IT staff. You wonder how to bridge the gap between your instructors' skills and the skills students bring with them to the classroom. There's not enough money to train the instructors and, even if your budget was not a concern, you wonder how and when the instructors would be trained. You also wonder if the students could help with technology needs.

Given this situation, how would you...

- Advance your instructors' technology skills?
- Find out if students can facilitate the use of more up-to-date technology in the classroom for their peers ? If so, how could this be accomplished?
- Determine what skills your instructors do and do not have with respect to technology?

Program Assessment

It's program assessment time and, as a new administrator, you've just been told that your college has not regularly reviewed or assessed its programs. You decide to check on your college's program outcomes which reveal some of your programs have no outcomes, other programs have only one to two, and the majority of the outcomes are not stated in program outcome terms. Your first thought is to panic because the institution's external accreditation visit is just short of three years away. You assess the reality of your decision and decide to tackle this issue head-on. What do you do?

1. What documents might exist to help you begin assessing the programs?
2. How should faculty become involved and engaged in this process?
3. What steps will be taken to revise existing program outcomes?
4. How will evidence from courses be collected to address whether or not program outcomes are met? Who will gather the evidence? Where will it be stored once gathered?

REFERENCES

Developmental Education FAQs. (n.d.). Retrieved from https://postsecondaryreadiness.org/developmental-education-faqs/

Schak, O., Metzger, I., Bass, J., McCann, C., & English, J. (2017). *Developmental Education: Challenges and Strategies for Reform*. Retrieved from https://www2.ed.gov/about/offices/list/opepd/education-strategies.pdf

Chapter 6

For Instructors:
Changing Teaching Styles to Accommodate All Learners

ABSTRACT

By now, you're hopefully up to your head in theory and have a good handle of where we've been. Now, the authors take you on a different kind of journey, to a place of the future. All bluster aside, there is merit behind grounding yourself in theory (as you no doubt know). In this chapter, they present the major takeaways for instructors. Before they get into these strategies to better assist your learners, they would strongly recommend that you have at least a basic understanding of Backwards Design and Fink's Integrated Teaching Approach. Both of these strategies will help you to design a class that is truly intentional and create a solid foundation for all of the tips and strategies they present. With each tip they provide a small piece of the puzzle that will ultimately help you to engage your learners in a way that provides more learner satisfaction, soft skill development, and helps your evaluations.

DOI: 10.4018/978-1-7998-0145-0.ch006

Copyright © 2020, IGI Global. Copying or distributing in print or electronic forms without written permission of IGI Global is prohibited.

INTRODUCTION

By now, your head is filled with theory, and you have a healthy understanding of where we've been. In this chapter, we'd like to take you on a different kind of journey, to a place of the future. All bluster aside, and, as you no doubt know, there is merit behind grounding yourself in theory. This chapter presents the major strategies instructors should consider to enhance their own and their post-traditional learners' experiences.

Before we examine these strategies, we strongly recommend that you have at least a basic understanding of Backwards Design (1949) and Fink's Integrated Teaching Approach (2003). Both of these strategies will help you to design a class that is truly intentional and create a solid foundation for the tips and strategies we present. Consider each tip a small piece of the puzzle that will ultimately help you to engage your learners in a way that provides more learner satisfaction, soft skill development, and help boost learner evaluations.

Gleaning Facts from Theory

In the former chapters that highlighted theory, we provided several ideas or tips useful for engaging post-traditional learners. Here's a quick review of these helpful tips.

Letting Learners choose their own Paths

By allowing learners to decide their own path, whether through flexibility in learning activities or engaging in discourse regarding the syllabus, empowering your learners to be a part of the learning experience changes learner experiences and teaching practices for the better.

Through Knowles (1980), we know our learners need to be generally self-directing. As an instructor, the easiest way to engage learners in choosing their own path is curriculum flexibility, realistic learning activities, teaching method variability, and empowering the learners.

Negotiate Your Curriculum

Curriculum flexibility is one of the first areas where you can really enact a change for your post-traditional learners. We hope that many learners see instructors as a guide and content facilitator, rather than as an authoritative figure that simply tells. On day one of your class, a suggestion is to negotiate assignment and assessment expectations with your learners. We speak about how every learner is different, yet, in many higher education courses, we don't seem to acknowledge this difference as a core foundation when deciding what to teach and the best approaches to deliver the content. When you first design the class and its syllabus, consider how learners can demonstrate what they've learned. This can be accomplished through multiple types of assessments. One of our former mentors told a story about how, for years, learners in his class preferred an oral presentation for their final assessment. It was not until recently, this mentor had a group of learners who wanted to be assessed through a written exam. By negotiating aspects of your curriculum, you empower learners and learn a lot about what they bring to the classroom. If you have learners, who are working full-time or have other full time roles like parenting, negotiating deadlines and other ways for them to exhibit content competency can help to ease some of the pressure that exist due to multiple responsibilities and time demands. This negotiation can work with any type of learner, as it allows for flexibility, which is often missing in higher education, but still provides a structured format. It's been our experience that learners with multiple responsibilities and, especially graduate learners attending conferences, will greatly appreciate you.

Learning Activities

Learners having various ways of making meaning in their lives. Due to this, assignments and teaching methods can either be intentionally designed for learners or have a layer of arbitrary standards. Consider your current style. Do you use the same type of assignment for the majority of your learning activities, i.e., reflections, quizzes, essays? As you develop your course content, simultaneously consider how the learning assessments could interact with different types of activities. Reflect on how well a selected assessment aligns to the content. Contemplate building active learning into the activity as well as the assessment.

One way to think outside of our preferred learning activity type is to consult Bloom's Taxonomy (1956). We motioned Bloom's (1956) work in a previous chapter. As you develop your course, you may initially desire learners recognize terms. As the weeks progress, the learning should be scaffolded. For example, you want your learners to recognize the terms but also to apply them to new situations. For the recognize phase, you could give your learners a quiz consisting of multiple choice or matching questions. Another suggestion to assess learners' recognition of the terms is to have the learners work in pairs then, using a tracking checklist, walk around the classroom and listen to the learners' use of the terms. It's true that a quiz will allow you to know if the learners retained the term knowledge, at least for that moment in time. But, as a passive activity, it doesn't allow for deeper levels of meaning and learners will eventually forget the terms if they do not regularly put them into some form of context and practice. If a simple, quick check of knowledge is all you're looking for, then the quiz is your method, but research done by Stains et al. (2018) shows that even in our hard sciences and STEM fields, active learning outperforms passive learning.

Teaching Method Variability

Negotiating the syllabus and varying learning activities will help post-traditional learners to feel a sense of engagement; however, it is the choice of teaching methods that will help you reach the largest numbers and, hopefully, all of your learners in the class. When considering teaching methods, there are few pieces of research that are relevant. First, the active learning piece shared earlier. Our learners, per Freeman et al. (2014) engage better with active learning methods rather than passive learning. Your first stop should be to aim at the types of methods that will engage your class in both critical and intentional ways. This includes using classroom dialogues, in-class peer group work, flipped classrooms, case studies, demonstrations, and problem-based learning. Using a variety of different teaching methods can help learners stay engaged with the material. Choi, Raymond and Hentschel (2018) found, that by incorporating service learning into the course, the learners' richness and depth of understanding increased; however, their fractural knowledge did not increase. (Note: This study was in Gerontology, so fractural knowledge referred to the specific knowledge they were attempting to gain. In short, fractural is not a typo.) Research will continue to find ways to increase knowledge comprehension. Until we know how best to enact this outcome, engage learners so they feel more involved with and have a better understanding of the content and the context surrounding it. By aiming for methods that better support learners' active engagement in material, learner satisfaction, soft skill gain, and potentially course evaluations will all increase.

Empowering Your Learners

Your learners are human and require several considerations to truly be successful. We've already talked about negotiating your syllabus, but this is where Tinto (2016) and his emphasis on self-efficacy are advantageous. Your learners need to feel acknowledged. Our role as instructors is not simply to disseminate information. With the changes in technology, instructors can find almost anything on the internet including tutorials that show how to complete a task. Thus, as instructors, the task has shifted away from simply disseminating knowledge to empowering our learners through soft-skill gains, including communication and critical thinking, along with knowledge to be successful. To this end, one approach would be to provide learners with smaller projects at the beginning of the class. This engages your learners in the first few assignments and activities and moves learners to the outcome of helping them understand the class, how the course and content fit in the "real" world, and the expectations they need to follow. By doing so, a large amount of learner anxiety will decrease allowing them to begin to move toward a sense of belonging and self-efficacy. This, in turn, is similar to a learner orientation to learning, because it allows learners to feel like they're creating their own path and understanding the present environment.

The Role of Experience

Well-designed classes that incorporate opportunities for reflection and use of previous experience increase learner satisfaction, as well as knowledge retention (Stains, et al., 2018).

The role of experience cannot be understated. These words should echo in your head as you build your class. We previously emphasized the importance of active learning, but there are more pieces to discover that will help you develop active experiences for your learners. The next piece we'll discuss is incorporating learner experience.

Incorporating Learner Experience

Learners, regardless of their background, have plentiful experiences upon entering the classroom. Some opponents may argue that traditional learners bring little experience with them to the classroom. It's been our lived experience that engaging traditional and post-traditional learners in active learning exercises allows for a sharing of two very different worlds, both rich with eperience. The adage by Otto von Bismarck which states, "A fool learns from their own mistakes. A wise man [person] learns from the mistakes of others". (Goodreads, n.d.) is a great way to subscribe to post-traditional learners' experiences. By incorporating knowledge from outside the classroom, both traditional and post-traditional learners gain new insights from each other, which may help to build a sense of camaraderie. And, this camaraderie is helpful to the success of new learners. Formerly, we mentioned that a sense of belonging is one of the needs Tinto (2016) stressed in his newest work on learner persistence.

Readiness to Learn

One of the major reasons for a historical approach to theory is to help create a better understanding of how much we know, and how much we can help our learners grow, that is, if we pay attention to previous theory and its updates.

Our learners are unique, diverse, and above all, we believe, hungry for knowledge. This hunger for knowledge drives our learners, as they are in a position to immediately acquire and apply knowledge. Working in a department of Educational Leadership that housed both an Adult and Higher Education (AHED) and K-12 program, one of your authors saw a fair share of learners who had been out in the workforce. Most were principals ready for the next phase of their learning. These learners brought incredibly diverse experiences, as well as backgrounds in human resources, leadership, supervision, and budgets. In the classroom, these learners engaged at every turn which helped the learners, who had less work experience, to apply the content. When you imagine your learners, do you imagine them as an eighteen-year-old and directly out of high school? Or, do you see your learners with a wealth of experience, ready to contribute? This leads us to our next tip on engaging your learners, "strike while the iron is hot".

Strike While The Iron Is Hot

In short, be ready and enthusiastic on day one. We've all been handed the class a day before it started, because of [you insert whatever ridiculous reason]. However, our first impression and how we present the material makes a difference in the learners' perspectives of the class. This includes acting like you know what's going on from day one, even if you've just learned you would teach the class. We cannot stress this enough. Often, new instructors will make a statement like "I don't consider myself an expert; I'm learning along with you." While that is realistic and quite humble, learners are looking to you as the content expert. They do not know that the day before the class started you were handed the class, nor should they. In some manner they are paying for the class and expect you to teach them. While you may not have previously taught the class and the course may not be your preferred specialty area, you DO have content knowledge and experiences. On the same topic, we're not suggesting that you will know everything. It is absolutely acceptable to admit you don't know answers to some questions. What's more important is how you approach not knowing the answer. Make sure to write questions down and get your learners the information they need after class or as soon as you can. In summation, act prepared and exhume enthusiasm for the subject matter. Learners will quickly pick up on whether you care about the content or not and them.

Orientation to Learning

The skills learners gain in the classroom need to be much more about tangible steps they can take to solve real life issues, rather than a curriculum exclusively designed to engage in a theoretical discussion.

We've covered several major points in the previous tips, but let's focus in on what makes a curriculum viable to current learners and how this interacts with learners' roles.

Curriculum Viability

While we are huge fans of theoretical models and approaches (Source: This entire book), your learners need a more realistic approach to your curriculum. Using real life events, case studies, and in-depth discussions on topics and how the topics relate to authentic activities will help learners gain motivation in the classroom, as well as a deeper understanding of the topic. Learning assessments that require your learners to think more critically about the content provides another characteristic of learning. Although an assessment, like a selected-response exam or quiz can be used, these assessments may miss the learning mark. Why? They typically don't ask learners to analyze, synthesize or evaluate the information. They tend to assess only lower-levels of learners' understandings. Projects that require learner reflection, like problem-based learning, labs that require hands-on experiences, or assessments that require learners to synthesize and/or evaluate their work become powerful tools to develop higher-order thinking skills.

Providing Opportunities to Share Roles

Learners are invested in their success, but that doesn't mean that being a learner is their only role. We mentioned it before. Part of the reason we used the term "learner" instead of "student" is because of the connotation brought forward by the word "learner". When you refer to someone as a learner, generally, that is considered their priority or perhaps sole role. Post-traditional learners are attempting to learn while also navigating their roles as breadwinner, community members, parents, and the list goes on. When designing your learning activities and assessments, provide opportunities for reflection that allow your learners to use their real-life experiences. This may involve calling upon examples from an organization the learners are part of to help you better explain the content. If the class has a research expectation, have the learners use their place of work, volunteer organizations, or the institution as part of the research. You can assist learners to take something back with them to their organizations or promote critical thinking on topics by attaching tangible items to the more theoretical concepts. In doing this, you allow for a balance of multiple roles, while helping learners see the relevance and value of the material. In turn, learners will produce more self-efficacy.

Motivation to Learn

The classroom is one of the most powerful areas for learner growth. A learners' ability to truly enjoy education rests in your hands. This isn't designed to scare you, but pulling questions from a test bank or using slideshows from predecessors may get you through the class, but your learners will feel the same way. They will do the work to pass, yet the desire to learn may be lost when confronted with experiences that either emphasize only externally motivating factors or disallow learners to pursue their intrinsic motivations.

Learner motivation has been previously discussed so we won't repeat it all again; however, there are several factors to consider when designing your class, including optional assignments, adhering to your curriculum, and leveraging the growth mindset.

Optional Assignments

While there's a general tendency to focus on struggling learners or those performing the bare minimum, we rarely talk about learners who go above and beyond in the classroom. When considering your class design, what types of content do you offer in your class for learners who want to go *beyond* the curriculum in the course? Often, our post-traditional learners are yearning for information because it's pertinent and relevant to their other roles. As you create assignments, consider optional assignments in the following ways:

1. Assignments for different types of learner engagement - You know that you'll have learners from multiple backgrounds. This statement especially applies to persons teaching in liberal arts curriculums, as these learners will have less sense of how a class, which is outside their anticipated degree field, can benefit them. Consider allowing learners to turn in assignments through multiple formats. For example, instead of only allowing a paper, permit learners to submit a video or a presentation over the same assignment. Learners will be more motivated and engaged when allowed to have a choice in how to complete the assignment. We can hear some of you saying but that means not everyone will complete the same assignment. The focus should not be on the format of an assignment, rather the focus should be on how well your learners met an assignment's outcomes. If the outcomes are the same, regardless of the assignment's format, we would argue that your learners are learning what you set out for them to learn.

2. Assignments for those who wish for mastery - As stated before, some learners want or need to know everything about a topic and are hungry for new knowledge. By using current events or recent findings, challenge learners to go above and beyond the given curriculum to better understand

how the content fits into real life. While extra credit can be provided as an incentive, it does not have to be required. Many learners will simply engage because they want to know more. Yes, this really is true; we've experienced it.

Adhering to Your Curriculum and Schedule, Until You Don't

One of the other important areas surrounding motivation is how your curriculum is viewed by your learners, and how well you stick to that curriculum. By working with your learners on the first day to establish aspects of the curriculum, you can avoid several issues that may come into play later on in the term. If you wish to change something in the course curriculum, a general rule is do not be wishy-washy with your expectations regarding the change. If the change is going to add more work for your learners, strongly consider implementing it the next time you teach the class or reduce other assignments to offset the added work. Learner motivation is a cornerstone of an effective class. Influences like ambiguous expectations and directions, changing of assignments, unclear assessments, pop (penalty) quizzes, and assessing learners on information that you did not assign, will create a sense of anxiety, which can lead to feelings of less self-efficacy, and learners feeling demotivated.

Leveraging the Growth Mindset

Psychology has given us a treasure trove of information on learner behavior. One of the most important treasures is the concept of the growth mindset. Primarily emphasized by Dweck (2006), the growth mindset posits that your learners can have either a fixed mindset or growth mindset when they're approaching a subject. Those who have a fixed mindset believe that abilities, aptitude, and traits are all innate, and thus they can only work within in their means. For our learners, this manifests in emphasizing activities they consider themselves "good at", and relegating learners to other "lower aptitude" areas to be deemphasized. If you've heard, "I'm just not good at…" this is a pretty clear example of learners who are stuck in a fixed mindset. Compared to a learner who believes in the growth mindset, you may hear something like, "I haven't spent a lot of time on this topic. I need to dedicate more time to it". This subtle change in speech emphasizes what a learner knows about themselves.

It tells us the learners that will "always be bad at x", or that through hard work and dedication, they can become better in an area they may currently lack. It's important to note that this is not the same as intelligence. Not every learner that comes into your classroom will have the same aptitude; however, their understanding of what they need to do to succeed is something you can leverage. We can generally use our first interaction with learners to explore this difference. You wouldn't believe the difference it makes when a learner who has low self-efficacy and believes they are just "not good at this" finds out that part of the reason they continue to "not be good in an area" is because of their mindset. This is especially helpful for learners who have struggled in the past or have been told they aren't smart by peers, family members, or, we dislike saying this, previous instructors. By being explicit in your initial interaction with learners about how they can succeed, the doorway is open to more learner success. While not every learner will be in a place to tackle the topic to their fullest, this provides a building block to success.

Self-Directed Learning

Being a master of your own education means serving as a guide and support for those who are working their way through higher education. This includes continuing to play a supportive role in learners' growth, both as a mentor and instructor.

We know that a majority of learning takes place outside the classroom. Assuming this, how then do we provide learners with the opportunity to use the skills they've developed while out of school? The answer lies in the content which is selected to engage your learners.

Learner Class Content

Learners who have been juggling multiple roles know the value of time and are more apt to speak out when given what they perceive as "busy work". We describe busy work as assignments that take up a lot of time but don't have real-world relevance. Some instructors employ this method to get to the required number of clock hours expected for the course, but, in reality, these assignments tend to waste the learners' and the instructor's time. To avoid the busy work trap, our recommendation is two-fold. First, make sure you're creating learning activities that emphasize ease of access and real-life application. Self-directed learners won't like trick questions, tiny verbiage changes that completely change the sentence, or ambiguity. These learners prefer direct and explicit content and directions. As instructors, we need to be mindful of these not so helpful teaching practices. Second, classroom activities, teaching methods, learning activities, and assessments should be clear to learners at the onset of the instruction. Both of your authors have encountered professors who believe that ambiguity in an assignment equates to critical thinking and soft skill development. We know better. Ambiguity does not provide an increase in critical thinking but, we believe, may lead to learners' excess stress and anxiety. The lack of knowing what an instructor is looking for on an assignment creates a negative culture, and detracts learners from attempting to get the most out of a class on their terms. We suggest developing outcomes, using Bloom's Taxonomy (2001) and designing rubrics or stating clear criteria for assignments that specifically align with the outcomes. Criteria should allow learners to understand exactly what is expected of them. It should indicate a clear target. Doing so, is not handholding, nor making assignments too easy. The opposite is true. It's removing arbitrary difficulties and replacing them with intentional learning.

Tinto's Retention Theory

Many of our strategies revolve around the idea of risk factors and retention. As an instructor, you have the ability to influence a learner's sense of belonging, value of the curriculum, and self-efficacy. These are all important concepts that add to learners' overall experiences in higher education and provide motivators for their classroom work.

The past decade has helped us to understand how to influence not only learner understanding, but also learner persistence in higher education. From the instructional side, let's consider the ways in which we can apply learners' self-efficacy, sense of belonging, and value of the curriculum.

Self-Efficacy, Imposter Syndrome, and You

We've highlighted this concept in several other areas, but it absolutely needs to have its own section. Self-efficacy is a driving force behind learner persistence. When learners feel strong self-efficacy, they can climb almost any mountain you give them! Be careful, though, not to make arbitrarily hard mountains for the sake of arbitrariness. To help your learners climb that mountain, it's helpful to know that your learners value your feedback, acknowledgement and encouragement. When grading, make sure to provide positive and **specific** feedback. Saying "good job" is positive but it tells learners very little about what was good about the work they performed. Instead, be explicit with the feedback so learners know what to continue to do versus what they need to improve. Some people use the sandwich approach (positive, negative, positive) to provide feedback, although there may be a tendency for learners to hear (eat) only the negative part of the sandwich. If you're new to the idea of giving feedback, the sandwich approach may help you get started. In summary, by emphasizing their success, learners feel acknowledged and are more apt to tackle difficult problems they may encounter in the future.

Self-efficacy relates to a learner's imposter syndrome. Clance and Imes (1978) first coined the term, then Clance (1985) delved further into the topic, by detailing and designing a measurement tool to understand imposter syndrome. Those who suffer from imposter syndrome feel like the accomplishments they achieve are a result of things like luck, rather than their own ability, hard work, and skill. Among our incoming learner populations, Black learners who reported imposter syndrome also reported "...higher levels of anxiety, as well as depression related to the discrimination they perceived" (https://www. insidehighered.com/news/2017/04/06/study-shows-impostor-syndromes-effect-minority-learners-mental-health). This includes first generation learners and learners from lower socio-economic backgrounds. Ramsey and Brown (2018), explain that populations from ethnic minorities, first generation learners, and women in specific fields are prone to suffer from imposter syndrome. "While this research indicates myriad factors influencing the lower overall retention rates for these groups, imposter syndrome may certainly be counted among them" (Ramsey & Brown, 2018, p. 1).

With the changing demographics we discussed in earlier chapters, our learners may very well come from these diverse backgrounds. When working with your learners, remember that you have the capacity to be a mentor, even if you do not see yourself as one. Your learners will rely on you both, personally and professionally, for advice. Understanding your higher education institutions' services such as career services, academic advising, counseling, writing center and other academic or personal services, will help you support your learners. You do not and should not be the landing spot for all matters regarding your learners, instead referring learners to the correct resources will best support those learners who may be suffering from imposter syndrome.

Transformative Learning

Let's take a step back and really design a solid teaching experience that emphasizes learner development that will not only help your end-of-the term evaluations, but will truly provide an experience where learners can challenge their own norms, assumptions, and depart from your class with a better worldview than before the class.

Change is constant which means our learners consistently change. Within a single class, learners may be challenged in ways they never thought possible. They may be able to break through prior norms and establish new ways of making meaning. Knowing this, instructors can position content to allow learners to explore.

Challenge and Support

A cornerstone of the student affairs world, challenge and support, is a fundamental goal that instructors should emphasize. When designing learning activities, position material to provide learners the opportunity to both discuss and debate content. If we were to look at this through Perry's theory (1970), we know that our learners can be at varying points in their journey in both their academic and personal lives. Learning activities that provoke thought and debate on subjects can allow learners to move from dualism to multiplicity, multiplicity to relativism, and to full commitment. By creating discussion surrounding a topic, learners may not only learn about a concept, but they may also work through Mezirow's 10 steps, and perhaps even achieve a new stage in their intellectual journey (Mezirow, 1997).

Learning Outcomes - Intellectual Development

Have you met an instructor who clearly explained the content but nothing more? The entirety of the class was dedicated to disseminating knowledge and you memorizing then regurgitating the information. This older and, what we would say is a traditional teaching style, is not as relevant today as it once was. Why? Hop online where you will find many examples of people explaining similar content. We are not advocating that all online information is accurate nor that finding online content can substitute for the course instructor.

However, we are advocating for instructors to consider their course learning outcomes and develop ones that emphasize intellectual development. While it may be tempting to focus solely on learning outcomes that cover the major topics you prefer to discuss in the class, including a learning outcome that emphasizes assisting learners on their intellectual journey will help them to achieve a more holistic worldview and allow you to focus your content and teaching on your learners.

Chapter Six Conclusion

This chapter provided different ways to engage learners. Utilizing a well-designed curriculum centered on theory that emphasizes the learners' needs is a fantastic way to start redesigning your course curriculum to better serve post-traditional learners. You are almost to the chapter case study. It represents the opportunity to consider how you would work with both instructors and administrators in your position. Using the chapter's information and, after reading through the scenario, answer the prompts. Keep in mind that you have an opportunity to build a narrative supporting your post-traditional learners!

Case Study: Teamwork Makes the Dream Work!

You work at a small, private college in the Midwest. With an enrollment of roughly 1,500 students, your institution emphasizes a 70-20-10 load, that is, 70% teaching, 20% research and 10% service. The average age of your learners is 29-years-old, with over half of the learners married and having at least one child. Three months ago, your university hired a new president. Your new president has taken issue with the siloing that is present on campus and, thus developed a new initiative with two main goals. The first goal is to bridge the existing gaps between student affairs and academic affairs. The second goals is to integrate the varied academic departments to increase cohesion and the dissemination of different teaching methods across the campus.

Scenario 1

You are currently paired with a new instructor from a different department at the university. This instructor finished her doctorate in the spring and started working for the university in the fall. As a novel instructor, you could describe her as exhibiting "unrefined enthusiasm". After meeting several times, it's clear the professor is excited, but clearly inexperienced in her approach to teaching.

- What kind of ways can you start to mentor this instructor?
- As this person is in another department, what challenges could you face with departmental teaching styles?

Scenario 2

You find yourself paired with a veteran administrator. This person has been at the university for a long time. You attempt to schedule several meetings, but find the long-term administrator is less than enthused to schedule a time. When the meeting finally takes place, unpleasant is the best word you can describe for the interaction that occurred. The administrator is abrasive, and bristles at the thought of post-traditional learners and needs for policy change. "We've always done it this way, it's just a new fad." After the conversation, you leave quite frustrated, but determined to at least be heard. As this is the president's initiative, you need to continue to meet with this administrator.

- What facts or statistics could you find and bring to the next meeting to help explain that this is not "just a new fad."
- When faced with someone who refuses to believe in new ideas, what tactics could you use to showcase potential losses to the institution if policies aren't changed?

Scenario 3

As part of the exchange between departments, you are elected to provide information on policies and instruction to another department. As you prepare the presentation, post-traditional learners' needs form the basis of your policies and instruction.

- If you had a "wish list" of both policies and instructional methods, what would be your preferred items for your university?
- If you had ten minutes to explain your top policies and instruction, what would you prioritize?
- If you could list only three priorities, what would they be?

REFERENCES

Bloom, B. S. (1956). *Taxonomy of educational objectives: The classification of educational goals* (1st ed.). Harlow, UK: Longman Group.

Choi, E., Raymond, J., & Hentschel, M. (2018). Facilitating Course Connections and Transitions to Project Closure in Service Learning. *Journal of Experiential Education*, *41*(4), 411–424. doi:10.1177/1053825918804570

Clance, P. R. (1985). *The Impostor Phenomenon: When Success Makes You Feel Like A Fake*. Atlanta, GA: Peachtree Publishers.

Clance, P. R., & Imes, S. A. (1978). The imposter phenomenon in high achieving women: Dynamics and therapeutic intervention. *Psychotherapy (Chicago, Ill.)*, *15*(3), 241–247. doi:10.1037/h0086006

Dweck, C. S. (2006). *Mindset: The new psychology of success*. New York: Random House.

Fink, L. D. (2003). *Creating significant learning experiences: An integrated approach to designing college courses*. San Francisco, CA: Jossey-Bass.

Freeman, S., Eddy, S., Mcdonough, M., Smith, M., Nnadozie, O., Jordt, H., & Wenderoth, M. (2014). Active learning increases student performance in science, engineering, and mathematics. *Proceedings of the National Academy of Sciences of the United States of America*, *111*(23), 8410–8415. doi:10.1073/pnas.1319030111 PMID:24821756

Good Reads. (n.d.). *Otto Von Bismark Quotes*. Retrieved from https://www.goodreads.com/quotes/294225-only-a-fool-learns-from-his-own-mistakes-the-wise

Knowles, M. (1980). The modern practice of adult education: From pedagogy to andragogy. New York, NY: Cambridge.

Mezirow, J. (1997). Transformative Learning: Theory to Practice. *New Directions for Adult and Continuing Education*, *1997*(74), 5–12. doi:10.1002/ace.7401

Perry, W. G., & Harvard University. (1970). *Forms of intellectual and ethical development in the college years: A scheme*. New York: Holt, Rinehart and Winston.

Ramsey, E., & Brown, D. (2018). Feeling like a fraud: Helping students renegotiate their academic identities. *College & Undergraduate Libraries*, *25*(1), 86–90. doi:10.1080/10691316.2017.1364080

Stains, M., Harshman, J., Barker, M. K., Chasteen, S. V., Cole, R., DeChenne-Peters, S. E., & Young, A. M. (2018). Anatomy of STEM teaching in North American universities. *Science*, *359*(6383), 1468–1470. doi:10.1126cience.aap8892 PMID:29599232

Tinto, V. (2016, September 26). From retention to persistence. *Inside Higher Ed*. Retrieved from https://www.insidehighered.com/views/2016/09/26/how-improve-student-persistence-and-completion-essay

Tyler, R. (1949). *Basic Principles of Curriculum and Instruction*. Chicago: The University of Chicago Press.

Chapter 7
Conclusion

ABSTRACT

This chapter represents concluding thoughts as well as a recap of some of the overarching critical recommendations from the book. This chapter includes takeaways from the theories presented, as well as takeaways from the instructor and administrator chapters. Finally, the authors wrap up the chapter and book with comments on research ideas for administrators and instructors. These research ideas represent potential ways for both administrators and instructors to help engage the post-traditional learner population and support further research.

CONCLUDING THOUGHTS

Before we get into a recap of the takeaways presented in this book, we wanted to put forth some concluding thoughts.

First and foremost, thank you for reading this book.

The amount of work required to publish a book is rewarding and challenging. Having someone take the time, even if they don't agree with all of the concepts is still validating. So, thank you, whoever you are. We intend to continue this work, update the theory presented in this book, and advocate for more research on post-traditional learners.

The work isn't done yet. It's not even close to being done.

While we have pockets of information regarding post-traditional learners, the bulk of the research comes from synthesizing other populations. To date, we can count roughly 100 peer reviewed articles that span post-traditional

DOI: 10.4018/978-1-7998-0145-0.ch007

Copyright © 2020, IGI Global. Copying or distributing in print or electronic forms without written permission of IGI Global is prohibited.

research. As an emerging area, you are in an unique position to not only assist post-traditional learners but enlighten the field. By documenting your changes in policies, programs, teaching methods, and services, you can support the research being conducted on the post-traditional population. For those who are in pre-K-12, or assist with these programs, consider this population when you're developing policies. In many states, the trend is moving from a pre-K-12 view to a pre-K-20 view, and there is merit in finding the "end goal" for your learners.

Publish And Present Work With Your Post-Traditional Learners

Whether you find yourself leaning towards quantitative, qualitative, or mixed-methods research, post-traditional learners will find success from your efforts to assist them. If you have the opportunity, speak regionally and nationally on post-traditional learners about your efforts to support them. We're sure you will be surprised by the amount of questions you get at conferences regarding this population and ways to best support with post-traditional learners.

Student Athletes And Post-Traditional Learners

While it's unexpected to add new information in the conclusion, there are a couple of research areas that could be immediately beneficial to post-traditional learners. Currently, one of your authors is pursuing the similarities between student athlete needs and post-traditional learner needs. One similarity with these two populations is the interaction between how we support student athletes and post-traditional learners. Here are a few early tidbits from a brief synthesis of existing research.

1. **Roles:** Student athletes and post-traditional learners are unique campus populations that have similar time demands due to their outside roles and academics.
    a. Student athletes balance the roles of learner and athlete, which comes with consistent outside obligations that may take precedence over their studies. While we wish this wasn't true, it can very much be the case. To stay in college, athletic scholarships require athletes to perform a myriad of activities not necessarily focused on education.

      b.   Post-traditional learners have to balance multiple responsibilities such as a wage-earning position, parenting, extended family care-taker, and their role as a learner. Similar to student athletes, these responsibilities can take precedence over their studies.

2.   **Developmental Education Needs:** Incoming student athletes are like any other population entering higher education for the first time. There are certain learners that require more support, potentially in the form of developmental education. The same is true for our post-traditional learner population, who may be far removed from their previous education experience. For both populations, the need for developmental education becomes of paramount importance.

      a.   For student athletes, some universities will work in partnership with the athletic department to design developmental education courses that work with the rigid timeframes surrounding athletes' schedules.

      b.   For post-traditional learners, there is a similar and prevalent need to create flexible courses that support post-traditional learners.

      c.   For both populations, the major problem is time. After all, there are twenty-four hours in a day no matter how many activities an athlete or post-traditional learner tries to complete in that twenty-four hour period. The external pressure from these learner's competing roles requires unique solutions to manage the issue of time.

3.   **The Need for Structure:** Post-traditional learners and student athletes benefit from what we like to call "flexible structure". Explicit expectations, combined with a willingness to work with learners during busy time periods will lead to success. At the end of the day, we want our learners to walk away from higher education with more knowledge and soft skills. For the two populations, achieving these goals will require more support from professionals and instructors.

Potential Research Areas

One of the greatest ways for post-traditional learners to be heard is through research. Often, people want to help, they just don't have the answers. If you are considering research, here are a few potential areas that could benefit post-traditional learners:

1. **Job Advancement and Higher Education:** While we know higher education often leads to higher potential job earnings, an area worth exploring is the relationship between field (or discipline) outcomes and work outcomes. Do the knowledge, skills and abilities of our institutional missions, visions and course outcomes align well with the specific needs of jobs for which we are preparing our learners? While some areas may more closely align to a career area, there can also be a disconnect between what is being talked about in the classroom and the translated skills or abilities for learners in their jobs. While we don't want to force every item in the classroom to be directly associated with career expectations, there's value for courses and universities when learners are able to provide evidence to their employers that they possess specific knowledge, skills and abilities. As we move to be more intentional with the way we're interacting with our learners, external stakeholders' needs must be at the forefront of this intentionality.

2. **Globalization and Post-Traditional Learner Outcomes** is another area that needs more research. Post-traditional learners are gaining necessary skills by re-entering education, but how do these skills translate to the world outside of that region, state, or nation? With a global economy and shrinking world due to technology, this will become a heightened topic of conversation. Although some of the work on globalization for adult learners is applicable, a gap exists in the literature on global education outcomes for post-traditional learners already in the workforce and re-entering higher education.

3. **Integration of Post-Traditional Learner Needs Into Current Programs and Policies:** While we presented you with best case scenarios and unlimited budgets for activities you can use with post-traditional learners, we realize that it isn't feasible to build something new dedicated only to the post-traditional learner population. Thus, we propose using existing and new research to transform your current policies and programs to make them more accessible to post-traditional learners. Often, post-traditional and adult learners are an afterthought in many policies or programs. This results in policies or programs that provide little to no support for this population. Conducting research on current policies and programs to better support post-traditional leaners' needs will help meet their needs, yours, and your institution.

4. **Pre-K-20 Education:** While you wouldn't traditionally consider this an area of research for a post-traditional learner, there exists the question of "what's next" on the education horizon. With changes to education

budgets, laws, and expectations, the shift to Pre-K-20 education has arrived. Use our book as a platform to dive into the world of Pre-K-20 education and the needs of post-traditional learners as your guidepost.

Each of these research areas represents a different facet of need for post-traditional learners. The more we identify specific needs at the administrative and instructor levels, the easier it will be for our learners to persist. If you're unsure of where to start, consider taking some time and reading more of the current literature on post-traditional learners. From there, your goal isn't to create a brand new theory (Unless you really want to, then go for it.); your goal is to move the body of literature in the right direction. This allows you to better serve your learners and provides another jumping point for other research to be developed.

Parting Advice

The past chapters have taken you through the current world of post-traditional learners and provided suggestions to work with and teach to this population. Hopefully, the chapters provided you with information to think about and engage your post-traditional population. Before we end the concluding chapter, here's a summary of the major takeaways from the book.

A Few Parting Takeaways For Our Readers

With a little tweaking, our theoretical past can inform the future.

1. Considering the emphasis in chapters two and three on theory, there's no doubt that we believe theory is the bedrock to inform successful policy and instruction. While we discussed several theorists' work that can help guide your post-traditional instruction and policy creation, you should actively seek updates to these theories. If you're someone who has an issue finding time to stay abreast of current research, we would urge you to do one or more of the following:
    - Schedule a one hour meeting each week with yourself. Use this time to browse through new articles. You would be surprised at how much new knowledge can be gained by only dedicating one hour a week.

- ○ Set aside a professional development budget to attend regional and national conferences. Not only are these conferences enlightening to learn about new and upcoming research, they also become a robust networking opportunity, which leads to our final suggestion.
- ○ Join the associations that are at the forefront of the research you want to master. Many associations have simple volunteer opportunities that can place you in a position to meet some of the current, best, and informed people in the association, and most likely in their field. By becoming aware of these notable people, you can watch whenever they release new research, offer workshops, and present at conferences. This awareness allows you to spend less time on your own trying to find applicable research.

2. Learning approaches can be incredibly helpful when groundwork is laid.
   - ○ One of the easy ways to build your class is by talking to other professors in the field about the type of learning approaches they're currently using. Certain fields often lean on specific learning approaches, and, thus, there is most likely a preferred path that will help your learners in their pursuit of education and with workforce expectations.

3. Administrators – You are both a primary and secondary influencer of post-traditional learner education.
   - ○ We cannot stress enough just how much difference you can make in post-traditional learners' experiences. Because they typically work full-time, post-traditional learners can identify with another person working full-time. That sense of kinship is paramount to learners' successes and helps them see you, the other full-time worker, as a partner in their educational journey. A few reminders:
   - ○ Make sure you engage post-traditional learners when you can. While you don't need to post yourself outside of every class, there is merit in making a few intentional stops over the course of the term to encounter the learners. When it comes to upper-level administrative positions. We have witnessed that some people believe in the "sanctity of the office". It is important to maintain a form of hierarchal power, but it's also important to use this power to effect positive change. Change be enacted by interacting with your post-traditional population!

- Plan for your post-traditional learner population on campus! Implement areas that are designed for working adults. Negotiate daycare and plan events that are in the evening or on weekends so your learners can stay engage on campus. Events that include the entire family should be the norm. Remember, a sense of community and belonging are part of what helps a learner stay on campus. Use those facts to your advantage as you help learners persist.
- Academic affairs – Make sure your policies are designed for working adults. We cannot stress enough that policies, which require these learners to make in-person visit during regular business hours (e.g. 8 a.m.-5 p.m.), experiencing long wait times for admittance or financial aid, become major barriers for your post-traditional learner population.
- Student affairs – Events, policies, and programming are all areas that can help or hinder post-traditional learners on their path to success. Make sure that you take a step back when developing or revisiting policy and ask yourself "If I were working full-time, is this feasible?" By doing so, you can better assist your learners as they try to navigate their work, family, and educational journey.

4. Instructors – You are the frontline when it comes to helping post-traditional learners succeed. Always keep this in the back of your mind as you develop your course, design your assignments, and create assessments.
    - Post-traditional learners are just like you. They hold positions that require them to balance multiple roles. If you work full-time at an institution, you may have teaching, research, and service expectations, you may have a family in addition to your full-time job, or, you may be an adjunct instructor in addition to your full-time position. Like you, your post-traditional learners are also trying to balance their multiple responsibilities. They are taking classes in addition to working and have many other responsibilities. While the rigor of your course should not be in question, the way in which you ask your learners to complete assignments is important. Make sure you provide your learners with schedules, in advance. Early scheduling will allow post-traditional learners to, if needed, move around their other obligations.
    - Develop assignments with flexibility in mind. As someone who works predominately with post-traditional learners, there are times when life takes precedence over a course activity or assignment.

Make sure that your courses are designed in a way that allows your learners to continuously move towards completion. Giving your learners two or three tests that form the bulk of the course grade may seem reasonable to you; however, we know our learners are working and are used to managing multiple and authentic tasks. Space out larger assignments to allow ample time for completion. Scaffold assignment requirements and provide prompt and specific feedback as your learners complete each part. Communicate assignment expectations early so learners can ask questions. Remember, your learners are there because they want to learn. How great is that! Respectfully consider your learners' requests as they negotiate with you on coursework.

◦ Well-designed courses will go a long way to build success for your post-traditional learners. If you haven't created courses with post-traditional learners in mind, we recommend you revisit Fink's (2001) integrated approach. Utilize Fink's sound advice to create your course, as well as the elements we put forth in this book to support post-traditional learners.

5. It takes everyone. It takes everyone to truly embody the best way to support post-traditional learners. If instructors and administrators have background on post-traditional learners and their needs, they tend to be more supportive and can help make changes in the lives of learners. Provide training for instructors and administrators on post-traditional learners. You can offer the training in the form of a certificate and offer a stipend for those who attend. You can design the trainings to include other unique populations. You can offer a book study to discuss some of the major takeaways brought forth in this book. Either way, getting people to buy into the idea of different needs can help your post-traditional learners receive the support they need.

6. Dealing with inflexibility. A second area that runs afoul of positive changes is hearing people say "we've always done it this way". To us, this is a frustrating statement when trying to implement positive changes for learners. When faced with change-resistors, our recommendation is to "show the blood". At one of the author's current institution, there's a lot of talk of about the idea of "show the blood". In short, when you're faced with a decision, such as a budget reduction, you need to show people exactly what is lost by taking that approach. For post-traditional learners, a strong reliance on a traditional teaching method, like lecture, and a lack of flexibility when it comes to assignments, leaves post-traditional

learners feeling a loss of self-efficacy and respect. These not-so-helpful practices may ultimately lead to your learners dropping out of classes and the institution. It's important to remember the difference between academic rigor and arbitrary rigor. You can remind your instructors of the difference in these two types of rigor. While your instructors may seem frustrated by the conversation, more often than not, they want to help their learners. They may not have considered how a teaching method or assignment method was perceived by their learners.

7. A need for explicitness. Recently, one of your authors conducted a structured literature review on teaching methods focused on adult learners in undergraduate classes. The need for "explicitness" was a recurring theme in the literature review. While covered in some capacity in earlier chapters, this is a notably common issue for all learners. Revisit policies and assignments to make sure they're explicit in their language. Remember, ambiguous assignments and expectations don't increase learner problem solving or soft skill development, instead, they frustrate learners as they attempt to navigate ambiguity. This is especially true for assignments. If you aren't currently sharing guidelines or rubrics for applicable assignments, how do your learners know what you expect of them? Check your policies, procedures, and assignments to make sure they're easily understood.

8. Respect, respect, respect. We've mentioned self-efficacy in this book, but, for many, learners respect is what they desire. As administrators and instructors, we often forget our learners are balancing several other roles. A moment that stood out for one of the authors was a professor speaking about his expectations for the class, the learning activities, and a weekly quiz. Prior to handing out the first quiz in the course, the professor discussed the rationale behind having a quiz each week. The rationale equated to a lack of respect, that is, the learners would not study on their own without an external motivator. This lack of respect for the learners became a lack of trust in the professor. Not surprisingly the semester was tumultuous, ending with some very unbecoming course evaluations. This professor's position denied the learners and their hunger for knowledge. The lesson to learn is not all learners will show up prepared; however, denying post-traditional learners' intrinsic motivation is demotivating in a class.

FINAL REMARKS

As we conclude this book, we want to emphasize that supporting post-traditional learners is a consistent process requiring time and dedication. The takeaways and tips we've provided can and will help your learners persist, but you cannot do this on your own. You will need support from many – institutional, departmental, colleagues, support services, and more. Remember that your learners are there because they chose to complete their higher education. You should be a supporter on their educational journey. All you have to do is make the decision to support your learners in the most positive way possible.

REFERENCES

Alesandrini, K., & Larson, L. (2002). Teachers Bridge to Constructivism. *The Clearing House: A Journal of Educational Strategies, Issues and Ideas*, *75*(3), 118–121. doi:10.1080/00098650209599249

Ambrose, S. A., Bridges, M. W., DiPietro, M., Lovett, M. C., & Norman, M. K. (2010). *How learning works: 7 research-based principles for smart teaching*. San Francisco, CA: Jossey-Bass.

American Psychological Association. (n.d.). *Education and socioeconomic status*. Retrieved from https://www.apa.org/pi/ses/resources/publications/factsheet-education.pdf

Anderson, T., Rourke, L., Garrison, D. R., & Archer, W. (2001). Assessing teaching presence in a computer conferencing context. *Journal of Asynchronous Learning Networks*, *5*(2), 1–17.

Armellini, A., & De Stefani, M. (2016). Social presence in the 21st century: An adjustment to the Community of Inquiry framework. *British Journal of Educational Technology*, *47*(6), 1202–1216. doi:10.1111/bjet.12302

Aslanian, C., & Cross, K. P. (1983). Adults as Learners: Increasing Participation and Facilitating Learning. *The Journal of Higher Education*, *54*(5), 587–589. doi:10.2307/1981634

Association of American Colleges & Universities. (2015, January 20). *Employers judge recent graduates ill-prepared for today's workplace, endorse broad and project-based learning as best preparation for career opportunity and long-term success.* Retrieved from http://www.aacu.org/press/press-rele ases/2015employerlearnersurveys

Auger, T. (2003, May). Student-centered reading: A review of the research on literature circles. *EPS Update Newsletter.* Retrieved from https://eps. schoolspecialty.com/EPS/media/Site-Resources/Downloads/articles/ Literature_Circles.pdf

Axelson, R. D., & Flick, A. (2010). Defining student engagement. *Change: The Magazine of Higher Learning, 43*(1), 38–43. doi:10.1080/00091383.2 011.533096

Bandura, A. (1977). Self-efficacy: Toward a unifying theory of behavioral change. *Psychological Review, 84*(2), 191–215. doi:10.1037/0033-295X.84.2.191 PMID:847061

Bigdeli, S. (2010). Affective learning: The anxiety construct in adult learners. *Procedia: Social and Behavioral Sciences, 9,* 674–678. doi:10.1016/j. sbspro.2010.12.216

Bloom, B. S. (1956). *Taxonomy of educational objectives: The classification of educational goals* (1st ed.). Harlow, Essex, England: Longman Group.

Bloom, B. S. (1968). Learning for mastery. *Evaluation Comment, 1*(2), 1-12.

Bloom, B. S. (1971). Mastery learning. In J. H. Block (Ed.), *Mastery learning: Theory and practice.* New York: Holt, Rinehart & Winston.

Boyington, B. (2017, September 20). See 20 years of tuition growth at national universities. *U.S. News.* Retrieved from https://www.usnews.com/education/ best-colleges/paying-for-college/articles/2017-09-20/see-20-years-of-tuition-growth-at-national-universities

Bruner, J. S. (1960). *The Process of education.* Cambridge, MA: Harvard University Press.

Bucks Institute for Education. (n.d.). Retrieved from www.pblworks.org

Burke-Vigeland, M., Broz, D., Thaler, M., Barber, C., Hickson, K., LoBello, T., . . . Rydell, S. (2011). *The Dynamics of Place in Higher Education*. Retrieved from https://www.gensler.com/research-insight/gensler-research-institute/the-dynamics-of-place-in-higher-education

Bye, D., Pushkar, D., & Conway, M. (2007). Motivation, Interest, and Positive Affect in Traditional and Nontraditional Undergraduate Students. *Adult Education Quarterly*, *57*(2), 141–158. doi:10.1177/0741713606294235

Choi, E., Raymond, J., & Hentschel, M. (2018). Facilitating Course Connections and Transitions to Project Closure in Service Learning. *Journal of Experiential Education*, *41*(4), 411–424. doi:10.1177/1053825918804570

Clance, P. R. (1985). *The Impostor Phenomenon: When Success Makes You Feel Like A Fake*. Atlanta, GA: Peachtree Publishers.

Clance, P. R., & Imes, S. A. (1978). The imposter phenomenon in high achieving women: Dynamics and therapeutic intervention. *Psychotherapy (Chicago, Ill.)*, *15*(3), 241–247. doi:10.1037/h0086006

Connor, M. L. (2007). *Andragogy and pedagogy*. Retrieved March 1, 2007, from http://agelesslearner.com/intros/andragogy.html

Creswell, J., & Poth, C. (2018). *Qualitative Inquiry and Research Design: Choosing Among Five Approaches* (Kindle Edition). Retrieved from Amazon.com

Deslisle, R. (1997). *How to use problem-based learning in the classroom*. Alexandria, VA: ASCD.

Dewey, J. (1922). Human nature and conduct. New York, NY: The Modern Library.

Donaldson, J. F., & Graham, S. (1999). A model of college outcomes for adults. *Adult Education Quarterly*, *50*(1), 24–40. doi:10.1177/074171369905000103

Driscoll, M. P. (2005). *Psychology of learning for instruction*. Boston: Pearson Allyn and Bacon.

Dweck, C. S. (2006). *Mindset: The new psychology of success*. New York: Random House.

EBSCO. (2018). Education Research Complete. *ERC*. Retrieved from https://www.ebsco.com/products/research-databases/education-research-complete

Edmonds, D. (2015, May 28). More Than Half of College Faculty Are Adjuncts: Should You Care? *Forbes*. Retrieved from https://www.forbes.com/sites/noodleeducation/2015/05/28/more-than-half-of-college-faculty-are-adjuncts-should-you-care/#6e791ca01600

Encyclopedia Brittanica. (2019, February 25). *Tabula rasa philosophy*. Retrieved from https://www.britannica.com/topic/tabula-rasa

ERIC. (2018). Frequently Asked Questions. *ERIC*. Retrieved from https://eric.ed.gov/?faq

Fink, L. D. (2003). *Creating significant learning experiences: An integrated approach to designing college courses*. San Francisco, CA: Jossey-Bass.

Fisher, R., & Ury, W. (2011). *Getting to Yes: Negotiating Agreement Without Giving In*. Penguin Books.

Freeman, S., Eddy, S., Mcdonough, M., Smith, M., Nnadozie, O., Jordt, H., & Wenderoth, M. (2014). Active learning increases student performance in science, engineering, and mathematics. *Proceedings of the National Academy of Sciences of the United States of America, 111*(23), 8410–8415. doi:10.1073/pnas.1319030111 PMID:24821756

Freire, P. (2000). *Pedagogy of the oppressed: 30th Anniversary Edition* (Kindle Edition). Retrieved from Amazon.com

Gaytan, J., & McEwen, B. C. (2007). Effective online instructional and assessment strategies. *American Journal of Distance Education, 21*(3), 117–123. doi:10.1080/08923640701341653

Gillespie, K. J., & Robertson, D. L. (2010). A guide to faculty development (2nd ed.). San Francisco, CA: Jossey-Bass.

Good Reads. (n.d.). *Otto Von Bismark Quotes*. Retrieved from https://www.goodreads.com/quotes/294225-only-a-fool-learns-from-his-own-mistakes-the-wise

Goubeaud, K., & Yan, W. (2004). Teacher educators' teaching methods, assessments, and grading: A comparison of higher education faculty's instructional practices. *Teacher Educator, 40*(1), 1–16. doi:10.1080/08878730409555348

Hake, B. (1999). Lifelong learning in late modernity: The challenges of society, organizations and individuals. *Adult Education Quarterly, 49*(2), 79–90. doi:10.1177/074171369904900201

Hall, K., Murphy, P., & Soler, J. (2008). *Pedagogy and practice: Culture and identities*. Los Angeles: SAGE.

Harris, W. J. (1980). *Comparative adult education; Practice, purpose and theory*. New York: Addison-Wesley Longman Limited.

Henson, K. T. (1980). Teaching Methods: Designs for Learning. *Theory into Practice, 19*(1), 2–5. doi:10.1080/00405848009542864

Hilarius, J. D., Herawati, S. H., & Newcomb, P. (2019). Enhancing different ethnicity science process skills: Problem-based learning through practicum and authentic assessment. *International Journal of Instruction, 12*(1), 1207–1222. doi:10.29333/iji.2019.12177a

Holmes, G., & Abington-Cooper, M. (2000). Pedagogy vs. Andragogy: A false Dichotomy. *The Journal of Technology Studies, 26*(2), 50–55. doi:10.21061/jots.v26i2.a.8

Huitt, W. (2009). *Constructivism. In Educational Psychology Interactive*. Valdosta, GA: Valdosta State University. Retrieved from http://www.edpsycinteractive.org/topics/cognition/construct.html

Jensen, L., & Allen, M. (1994). A synthesis of qualitative research on wellness-illness. *Qualitative Health Research, 4*(4), 349–369. doi:10.1177/104973239400400402

Knowles, M. (1980). The modern practice of adult education: From pedagogy to andragogy. New York, NY: Cambridge.

Kuh, G. D., Cruce, T. M., Shoup, R., Kinzie, J., & Gonyea, R. M. (2008). Unmasking the effects of student engagement on first-year college grades and persistence. *The Journal of Higher Education, 79*(5), 540–563. doi:10.1080/00221546.2008.11772116

Kuhlenschmidt, S. (2010). Issues in technology and faculty development. In K. J. Gillespie & L. Robertson (Eds.), *A Guide to Faculty Development* (2nd ed.; pp. 259–274). San Francisco, CA: Jossey-Bass.

Kuhn, T. (1962). *The Structure of Scientific Revolutions*. University of Chicago Press.

Lambert, J. L., & Fisher, J. L. (2013). Community of Inquiry framework: Establishing community in an online course. *Journal of Interactive Online Learning, 12*(1), 1–16.

Lanford, M., & Maruco, T. (2018). When Job Training Is Not Enough: The Cultivation of Social Capital in Career Academies. *American Educational Research Journal, 55*(3), 617–648. doi:10.3102/0002831217746107

Lindeman, E. (1926). *The meaning of adult education.* New York: New Republic, Inc.

Major, C. H., & Palmer, B. (2006). Reshaping Teaching and Learning: The Transformation of Faculty Pedagogical Content Knowledge. *Higher Education, 51*(4), 619–647. doi:10.100710734-004-1391-2

Martin, E., Prosser, M., Trigwell, K., Ramsden, P., & Benjamin, J. (2000). What university teachers teach and how they teach it. *Instructional Science, 28*(5), 387–412. doi:10.1023/A:1026559912774

Marzano, R. J. (2007). *The art and science of teaching: A comprehensive framework for effective instruction.* Alexandria, VA: ASCD.

Merriam, S. B., & Bierema, L. L. (2014). *Adult learning: Linking theory and practice* (Kindle Edition). Retrieved from Amazon.com

Merriam, S. B., Cafferella, R. S., & Baumgartner, L. M. (2007). *Jossey-Bass higher and adult education series. Learning in adulthood: A comprehensive guide* (3rd ed.). Hoboken, NJ: John Wiley and Sons, Inc.

Merriam-Webster. (2019). *Didactic.* Retrieved from https://www.merriam-webster.com/dictionary/didactic

Mezirow, J. (1991). *Transformative dimensions of adult learning.* San Francisco, CA: JosseyBass.

Mezirow, J. (1997). Transformative Learning: Theory to Practice. *New Directions for Adult and Continuing Education, 1997*(74), 5–12. doi:10.1002/ace.7401

Mezirow, J., & ... (2000). *Learning as transformation: Critical perspectives on a theory in progress.* San Francisco, CA: Jossey-Bass.

Middlecamp, C. H. (2005). The art of engagement. *Peer Review: Emerging Trends and Key Debates in Undergraduate Education, 7*(2), 17–20.

Mitchell, M., Leachman, M., & Masterson, K. (2017, August 23). A Lost Decade in Higher Education Funding. *Center on Budget and Policy Priorities.* Retrieved from https://www.cbpp.org/research/state-budget-and-tax/a-lost-decade-in-higher-education-funding

Monks, J., & Schmidt, R. (2011). The impact of class size on outcomes in higher education. *The B.E. Journal of Economic Analysis & Policy, 11*(1). doi:10.2202/1935-1682.2803

Murphy, P. (2008). Defining pedagogy. In K. Hall, P. Murphy, & J. Soler (Eds.), *Pedagogy and practice: Culture and identities* (pp. 28–39). London: Sage Publications.

National Center for Education Statistics. (2017). *Definitions and Data.* Retrieved from https://nces.ed.gov/pubs/web/97578e.asp

National Survey of Student Engagement. (2003). *National survey of student engagement 2003.* Retrieved from http://nsse.indiana.edu/2003_annual_report/pdf /NSSE_2003_Annual_Report.pdf

Pavlov, I. P. (1910). *The work of the digestive glands.* London: Griffin. Retrieved from https://archive.org/details/workofdigestiveg00pavlrich/page/n17

Perry, W. G., & Harvard University. (1970). *Forms of intellectual and ethical development in the college years: A scheme.* New York: Holt, Rinehart and Winston.

Peterson, M. W., & Einarson, M. K. (2001). What are colleges doing about student assessment? does it make a difference? *The Journal of Higher Education, 72*(6), 629–669. Retrieved from http://proxyweb.doane.edu/login?url=https://search-proquest-com.proxyweb.doane.edu/docview/2053 37548?accountid=28184

Pew Research Center. (2017, July 10). Sharp Partisan Divisions in Views of National Institutions. *Pew Research Center.* Retrieved from http://www.people-press.org/2017/07/10/sharp-partisan-divisions-in-views-of-national-institutions//

Piaget, J. (1932). *The moral judgment of the child.* London: Routledge & Kegan Paul.

Popper, K. (1963). *Science: Conjectures and Refutations.* Routledge.

Powell, K., Stephens Helm, J., Layne, M., & Ice, P. (2012). Quantifying online learning contact hours. *Administrative Issues Journal: Education, Practice, and Research, 2*(2), 80–93. doi:10.5929/2012.2.2.7

Qiang, Z. (2003). Internationalization of higher education: Towards a conceptual framework. *Policy Futures in America, 1*(2), 248–270. doi:10.2304/pfie.2003.1.2.5

Ramsey, E., & Brown, D. (2018). Feeling like a fraud: Helping students renegotiate their academic identities. *College & Undergraduate Libraries, 25*(1), 86–90. doi:10.1080/10691316.2017.1364080

Roberts, N. (2013). *Disorienting dilemmas: Their effects on learners, impact on performance, and implications for adult educators.* Retrieved from https://digitalcommons.fiu.edu/cgi/viewcontent.cgi?referer=https://www.google.com/&httpsredir=1&article=1249&context=sferc

Rosenshine, B. (2012, Spring). Research-based strategies that all teachers should know. American Educator, 12-19, 39.

Schak, O., Metzger, I., Bass, J., McCann, C., & English, J. (2017). *Developmental Education: Challenges and Strategies for Reform.* Retrieved from https://www2.ed.gov/about/offices/list/opepd/education-strategies.pdf

Shulman, L. (1986). Those who understand: Knowledge growth in teaching. *Educational Researcher, 15*(2), 4–14. doi:10.3102/0013189X015002004

Skinner, B. F. (1938). *The Behavior of Organisms: An Experimental Analysis.* New York: Appleton-Century.

Skinner, B. F. (1948). Superstition' in the pigeon. *Journal of Experimental Psychology, 38*(2), 168–172. doi:10.1037/h0055873 PMID:18913665

Soares, L. (2013). Post-traditional learners and the transformation of postsecondary education: A manifesto for college leaders. *American Council of Education.* Retrieved from http://www.acenet.edu/news-room/Documents/Post-Traditional-Learners.pdf

Sorcinelli, M. D., Austin, A. E., Eddy, P. L., & Beach, A. L. (2006). *Creating the future of faculty development: Learning from the past, understanding the present.* Boston, MA: Anker.

Stains, M., Harshman, J., Barker, M. K., Chasteen, S. V., Cole, R., DeChenne-Peters, S. E., & Young, A. M. (2018). Anatomy of STEM teaching in North American universities. *Science*, *359*(6383), 1468–1470. doi:10.1126cience.aap8892 PMID:29599232

Stiggins, R. (2007). Assessment through the student's eyes. *Educating the Whole Child*, *64*(8), 22–26.

Swan, K., Day, S. L., Bogle, L. R., & Matthews, D. B. (2014). A collaborative, design-based approach to improving an online program. *Internet and Higher Education*, *21*, 74–81. doi:10.1016/j.iheduc.2013.10.006

Swan, K., & Ice, P. (2010). The Community of Inquiry framework ten years later: Introduction to special issue. *Internet and Higher Education*, *13*(1-2), 1–4. doi:10.1016/j.iheduc.2009.11.003

Tinto, V. (1975). Dropout from Higher Education: A Theoretical Synthesis of Recent Research. *Review of Educational Research*, *45*(1), 89–125. doi:10.3102/00346543045001089

Tinto, V. (2016, September 26). From retention to persistence. *Inside Higher Ed*. Retrieved from https://www.insidehighered.com/views/2016/09/26/how-improve-student-persistence-and-completion-essay

Torres, C. A. (1994). Introduction. In *M. Escobar, A. L. Fernandez, & G. Guevara-Niebla (Eds.), Paulo Freire on higher education: A dialogue at the National University of Mexico* (pp. 1–25). Albany, NY: State University of New York Press.

Tough, A. (1981). *Learning without a teacher: A study of tasks and assistance during adult self-teaching projects*. Toronto: Ontario Institute for Studies in Education.

Tsai, C. Y., Li, Y. Y., & Cheng, Y. Y. (2016). The Relationships Among Adult Affective Factors, Engagement in Science, and Scientific Competencies. *Adult Education Quarterly*, *67*(1), 30–47. doi:10.1177/0741713616673148

Tyler, R. (1949). *Basic Principles of Curriculum and Instruction*. Chicago: The University of Chicago Press.

U.S. Department of Education. (2014). *Ed Performance & Accountability*. Retrieved from https://www2.ed.gov/about/reports/annual/nclbrpts.html

Vygotsky, L. S. (1978). *Mind in society: The development of higher psychological processes.* Harvard University Press.

Walsh, D., & Downe, S. (2005). Meta-synthesis method for qualitative research: A literature review. *Journal of Advanced Nursing, 50*(2), 204–211. doi:10.1111/j.1365-2648.2005.03380.x PMID:15788085

Wang, V. X. (2014). *Advanced Research in Adult Learning and Professional Development: Tools.* Trends, and Methodologies. doi:10.4018/978-1-4666-4615-5

Wang, V. X. (2014). *Advanced Research in Adult Learning and Professional Development: Tools.* Trends, and Methodologies. doi:10.4018/978-1-4666-4615-5

Watson, J. B., & Rayner, R. (1920). Conditioned emotional reactions. *Journal of Experimental Psychology, 3*(1), 1–14. doi:10.1037/h0069608

Wyatt, L. G. (2011). Nontraditional learner engagement: Increasing adult learner success and retention. *Journal of Continuing Higher Education, 59*(1), 10–20. doi:10.1080/07377363.2011.544977

Wyatt, L. G. (2011). Nontraditional learner engagement: Increasing adult learner success and retention. *Journal of Continuing Higher Education, 59*(1), 10–20. doi:10.1080/07377363.2011.544977

Zakrajsek, T. D. (2010). Important skills and knowledge. In A guide to faculty development (2nd ed.; pp. 83-98). San Francisco, CA: Jossey-Bass.

Chapter 8
Supplemental Case Studies

ABSTRACT

As the name implies, these are additional case studies you can use with your learners or yourself to reflect on ways to better serve your post-traditional learner population. Consider each of the following through either an instructor or administrator's eyes. While there are some that are written specifically for administrators or instructors, the majority of the case studies allow you to view the scenario from either lens. At the end of each case are several questions to provoke reflection and thought on the case study.

INTRODUCTION

As the name implies, this chapter provides additional case studies you can use with your learners, or, for yourself, to reflect on ways to better serve the post-traditional learner population.

Case Study 1: Student Affairs as an Undergraduate Degree

As one of the leading institutions in the nation, administration decided there is a need for an undergraduate degree in Higher Education Student Affairs (HESA) program. [What? We can dream, can't we?]. You are in charge of developing a comprehensive curriculum and policy for the program. Your institution believes this new program will be a huge success, in part, due to the learner demographics on campus. Currently, the average age of learners

DOI: 10.4018/978-1-7998-0145-0.ch008

Copyright © 2020, IGI Global. Copying or distributing in print or electronic forms without written permission of IGI Global is prohibited.

on campus is 28, with online learners' average age at 31. The wealth of incoming knowledge from post-traditional learners will be a perfect mix for theory in the degree, or, so you believe.

Question Set One

1) To build this program, what information or factors do you need to take into account regarding your current campus population?
2) Considering the items you generated in the first question, in what ways can you support your learners' unique needs in the curriculum?
3) You are in charge of the curriculum but also policy. In what ways could you leverage policy to create an inclusive program for post-traditional learners?

As you start to develop your curriculum, you feel pretty good about the curriculum having practicality, intentionality, and a design that aligns with the standards set forth by the National Association for Student Personnel Administrators (NASPA) and the American College Personnel Association (ACPA) in their Professional Competencies Areas for Student Affairs Professionals. After your initial work on the curriculum, you turn your attention to policies. Admittedly, this is the first time you've developed a full degree program, and you have no idea what to do regarding policies.

Question Set Two

1) What resources should you research to inform your policies?
   a) What institutional policies should be of focus?
   b) What theory or theories should you rely on to inform policy?
2) If the program is completely new, where can you find potential policies to help design an inclusive program that accommodates learners from all backgrounds?

You research and find several other HESA programs. You contact each program to gather the information you desire and use your knowledge of post-traditional learners to cater the policies to be as inclusive as possible to learners from different backgrounds. After the initial creation of the policies and procedures, you are set to meet with several senior administrators and veteran instructors to review and discuss the new curriculum and policies you've created. As Murphy's Law would have it, one of the veteran instructors placed on the review committee is a faculty member, who is known to dislike the division of student affairs and makes his dislike clear. In fact, in the meeting he blurts out that administrative bloat created by student affairs is the sole cause for financial issues on campus.

Question Set Three

1) In what ways could you work, one-on-one with this individual?
2) Politically, as well as ethically, how would you approach this situation to have the best chance of mitigating risk from this individual?
3) What evidence might you share with the veteran instructor to have him reconsider his view of student affairs and the new program?

Case Study 2: Toys for Tots

You currently work on a campus where there exists a large number of post-traditional learners. While there are some very progressive policies on campus, there has been a consistent, looming issue for the campus – lack of a day care. After a recent campus climate survey, close to 35% of the respondents indicated there was a lack of child care facilities in the local area. Several instructors stated their learners have missed class or had no other alternative but to bring their child(ren) to class in order to continue their education. While the majority of instructors are supportive of learners and allowing their children in the classroom, whenever possible, it's clear that this is a growing problem and one that may require institution intervention to support learners. You are put on a task force to investigate the question of child care. The outcome of the task force is to produce a comprehensive summary of the benefits and drawbacks to the institution.

1) Is it the institution's responsibility to provide child care services? Why or why not?
2) If the institution were to provide child care, what types of issues could arise? How could these issues be mitigated?
3) As administrators and instructors, if adequate child care for the learners means they have a better chance of persisting to complete their education, what would you do to support the effort to provide child care?

Case Study 3: Business Partnerships

Your campus has seen a decline in traditional age learners coming to campus. As a way to boost learner numbers and persistence, a couple of new programs were developed. These programs partner with local companies. In these partnerships, learners are provided a curriculum which culminates in a business analytics, marketing, or human resources certificate. After a year of the program, there is a very stable partnership between local businesses and the institution, culminating in an impressive 10% of the total enrolled learner population. However, despite the success of the program, over 30% of the enrolled population in the program are not completing the courses. Seeking to maximize learner persistence in the classroom, you are asked to identify the factors contributing to why learners are dropping out. You meet with several program instructors. They tell you there are clear differences in the knowledge, skills, and abilities expected for the program and the learners' preparation. While some learners engage well in the course content, several instructors have come to you stating that most of the learners are not ready for the rigor of courses. The program is benefitting your institution and business partners. It's a program you and the business partners want to succeed. If you can find how to address the gap between the learners and program expectations, you know the learners will perform more satisfactorily in their job functions and have a greater chance to advance in their careers.

1) As an administrator, what evidence would you need to gather to determine a gap exists between learners' knowledge and program outcomes? How would you address the gap that exists?
2) In what ways could the program be redesigned to allow for more hands-on skill use, that is, in what ways could someone obtaining a marketing certificate gain hands-on skills?
3) What, if any, changes should be made to the current certificate curriculum to better support learners with developmental needs?

Case Study 4: The Dreaded other Duties as Assigned

You are working at a university that has a multitude of programs, and a strong post-traditional learner population on campus. Mina has worked at the institution as part of the janitorial staff for several years and has become an acquaintance you regularly see. The institution provided tuition reimbursement for employees and Mina plans to take up to two classes per semester. Excited to begin her journey, in the first few weeks of the semester, she tells you each day how she is doing in her classes. However, halfway through the semester you notice she has not come to stop by for the daily chats. Finally, a few days later you catch her in the hall. You ask her how classes are going, but the look she gives you is one of defeat. "I can't keep going," Mina says to you. "But why? You inquire. "What's going on Mina? You were excited at the start of this semester." Mina looks at you nervously. "I...my supervisor told me that the classes are interfering with my job. If I keep going to class, I could lose my job." This is the exact opposite of a supportive situation.

1) What type of discovery questions should you ask?
2) Would you approach the supervisor? If so, what ways would be appropriate?

You decide that confronting the supervisor is a prudent next step. You ask Mina if she is all right with you intervening in the situation. She seems hesitant but agrees. You decide to ask Mina several questions about the time frame in which classes occur and how the time slots are currently affecting her work schedule. She tells you that both of her classes are in the middle of her current work schedule. She has offered to stay later to make up the hours, but her supervisor is very rigid about the hours she works. Understanding this situation could keep Mina from persisting, you head over to speak with her supervisor.

1) What types of questions could you ask to not begin the conversation on a negative tone?
2) Are there policies or procedures you should consider before talking to the supervisor?
3) Would a conversation with the HR department regarding employees taking classes be a proactive step?
4) How could you leverage each of the three previous questions to form a cohesive plan to work with the supervisor?

You head over and meet with the supervisor. You explain your current role and share your concern about Mina managing both work and course expectations. You state that you're worried about Mina persisting this semester and in future semesters. The supervisor explains to you that "it's next to impossible to change schedules." Feeling like this answer is vague, as well as seeing a shift in the supervisor's non-verbals, you pursue a bit further. "This is incredibly important for Mina, and I'm surprised to hear that there is little flexibility, considering HR's policies on those who work and take classes through the loyalty program." The supervisor eyes you, saying that the "schedules are set in stone, and I'm not going to change my schedule so she can be working when I'm not here."

1) At this point in the conversation, should you continue to pursue the issue?
2) Are there any identifiable buzz words that may point towards the reason for the schedule being impossible to change?
3) What could your next steps be?

Case Study 5: A Sick Child

You have recently started teaching an academic inquiry class for your institution. This class is part of a new initiative designed to help support learners in their journey through academics. The course includes your department's core knowledge content and information traditionally found in a freshman seminar. As you survey your first class, you note there are students from many backgrounds. As you get to know your students, you find there's a good mix of traditional and post-traditional learners in the classroom. Excited to integrate experiences from your post-traditional learners, you decide to form groups in class to complete several activities. While the grouping initially goes well, you are approached by one of the groups with a concern. A large project is due soon and the group explains that one of their members has been skipping the group meetings for the past two weeks. As a result, this group member has not contributed to their piece of the project.

You reach out to this student, who's been in class, but, not at the group meetings. After getting in contact with her, she sends the following e-mail.

Hello,

I am so sorry. I reached out to my group several times, but recently they stopped responding. My child has been sick with pneumonia for several weeks, and my mother can only watch her certain times of the day. I've been able to come to class because she can watch her, but the group won't work with me to meet at a different time. I want to do well in this class, but my child comes first. I can't do anything if my group members won't work with me.

Sincerely,

XXX

1) As an instructor, what is your first reaction to this case study?
2) When considering the whole group and the individual members, what would be a good course of action?
3) There is a strong sense of rigidity for this post-traditional learner from other group members. What could be done in your group expectations to better handle a situation like this in the future?

Case Study 6: Operation Education

Case study provide by Dr. Roger Schieferecke. He has served students in higher education for 25 years and held leadership roles in the areas of admissions, enrollment management, and early college programs. He currently serves as an Assistant Dean in the College of Education and Director of the Center for Student Success at Kansas State University. He holds a doctorate in education from the University of South Dakota.

Background:

Katie had plans of working toward her degree immediately following high school but a funny thing happened along the way, love. Katie met her future husband the summer following her senior year of high school. Mark was two years older and had just finished boot camp when they began dating and quickly chose to spend the rest of their lives together. Katie delayed going to college so she could be with Mark while he completed Infantry school. She was talented with technology and had a strong work ethic and quickly landed full-time clerical employment. Mark successfully completed infantry school and the two settled in on base.

Mark ultimately reenlisted with the decision to make a career out of the military. They were happily married and parents of beautiful twins. They were, for the most part, content with their position in life. Katie often thought about returning to school but doing so while raising small children was daunting. Plus, the family needed dual incomes to make ends meet. Ten years later, with encouragement of her family and co-workers, Katie enrolled in the local college on a part-time basis. She had to maintain her clerical job because the family was dependent on that income.

The local college is a tier 1 research university with an enrollment of 30,000. The promotional campaigns tout the institution as rigorous yet supportive. It all sounded good but as a first-generation, working adult, military spouse, Katie has numerous questions weighing on her mind.

Question Set One

1. What can you learn from Katie's background before enrolling at your institution.
2. What questions might Katie have?
3. What particular services should your institution provide to support Katie's success?
4. How do you successfully deploy those services so they are utilized?

Katie begins classes and although she is excited about the prospects of earning her degree, she doesn't really feel like she belongs. To begin with, her classmates at orientation weekend and in her freshman seminar class appear to be at least ten years younger. In fact, the instructor is probably younger. Katie wonders if there are any other students like her. At mid-term time, Katie reflects on her experience. Although difficult, she is happy with her decision to go back to school. She is finding it challenging, however, to maintain some type of balance between family, school, and work. When one area pulls harder, the others suffer. The biggest issue has been dealing with the effects of her husband's deployment. Katie has essentially been a single parent for the last three months. Sick kids have resulted in missed work and missed classes. She's had to step out of class when her husband calls as he is limited to the times he can call. The calls don't occur regularly. She hopes her faculty understand that she is not simply skipping or being disrespectful and that she wants to be in class.

Question Set Two

1. As the spouse of a deployed soldier, what additional issues are affecting Katie's educational experience?
2. How can you mitigate the issues revealed in the previous question to provide Katie with more support?

Katie finishes the semester with a 2.75 GPA. It is lower than what she expected but given the events of the semester, she is content. She knows she will need to show improvement as her degree program requires a 3.0 GPA to graduate. Katie also has to be strategic when she enrolls in particular classes as some are only offered on campus, specific semesters, and at times that conflict with work. To further complicate matters, there are rumors of a permanent change in location for her husband, Mark. When that happens, Katie will have to start the process over as her current institution doesn't have systems in place to complete her degree from a distance.

Question Set Three

1. What advice do you have for Katie?
2. What changes could be implemented at your institution to support students in similar situations as Katie?
3. Are there other special populations on your campus that may have unique needs?
4. Does your institution have unnecessary barriers to degree completion?
5. What does the new "traditional" student look like at your institution and are you supporting them appropriately?

Related Readings

To continue IGI Global's long-standing tradition of advancing innovation through emerging research, please find below a compiled list of recommended IGI Global book chapters and journal articles in the areas of adult learning, higher education, and pedagogy. These related readings will provide additional information and guidance to further enrich your knowledge and assist you with your own research.

Acevedo, M. M., & Roque, G. (2019). Resisting the Deprofessionalization of Instructional Design. In Y. Vovides & L. Lemus (Eds.), *Optimizing Instructional Design Methods in Higher Education* (pp. 9–26). Hershey, PA: IGI Global. doi:10.4018/978-1-5225-4975-8.ch002

Adams, L., & Shambaugh, N. (2019). Applying Instructional Design Guidelines for Community Health Programs in Health Education. In Y. Vovides & L. Lemus (Eds.), *Optimizing Instructional Design Methods in Higher Education* (pp. 101–128). Hershey, PA: IGI Global. doi:10.4018/978-1-5225-4975-8. ch006

Akella, N. (2019). Designing Caring and Inclusive Online Classroom Environments for Non-Traditional Learners: A Case Study Exploring the Andragogical Teaching and Learning Model. In L. Kyei-Blankson, J. Blankson, & E. Ntuli (Eds.), *Care and Culturally Responsive Pedagogy in Online Settings* (pp. 63–87). Hershey, PA: IGI Global. doi:10.4018/978-1-5225-7802-4.ch004

Aljafari, R. (2019). Self-Directed Learning Strategies in Adult Educational Contexts: Helping Students to Perceive Themselves as Having the Skills for Successful Learning. In F. Giuseffi (Ed.), *Self-Directed Learning Strategies in Adult Educational Contexts* (pp. 124–137). Hershey, PA: IGI Global. doi:10.4018/978-1-5225-8018-8.ch007

Andrews, J. L., & Taylor, J. E. (2017). Keeping Adult Education in the Mix: Using the Marketing Mix to Foster Viable and Sustainable Graduate Programs for Adult Learners. *International Journal of Technology and Educational Marketing*, 7(1), 26–37. doi:10.4018/IJTEM.2017010103

Artze-Vega, I., & Delgado, P. E. (2019). Supporting Faculty in Culturally Responsive Online Teaching: Transcending Challenges and Seizing Opportunities. In L. Kyei-Blankson, J. Blankson, & E. Ntuli (Eds.), *Care and Culturally Responsive Pedagogy in Online Settings* (pp. 22–40). Hershey, PA: IGI Global. doi:10.4018/978-1-5225-7802-4.ch002

Asunka, S. (2017). "We Had a Blast!": An Empirical Affirmation of Blended Learning as the Preferred Learning Mode for Adult Learners. *International Journal of Mobile and Blended Learning*, 9(3), 37–53. doi:10.4018/IJMBL.2017070104

Ausburn, L. J., Ausburn, F. B., & Kroutter, P. J. (2017). Influences of Gender and Computer Gaming Experience in Occupational Desktop Virtual Environments: A Cross-Case Analysis Study. In V. Wang (Ed.), *Adult Education and Vocational Training in the Digital Age* (pp. 200–216). Hershey, PA: IGI Global. doi:10.4018/978-1-5225-0929-5.ch012

Bamba, P. (2019). Framing the Role of Culture Reflecting on How Culture Affects Learners in Transformative Learning Settings: The Adult Learner Culture Defined. In D. Peltz & A. Clemons (Eds.), *Multicultural Andragogy for Transformative Learning* (pp. 30–44). Hershey, PA: IGI Global. doi:10.4018/978-1-5225-3474-7.ch003

Baran, M. L. (2019). Teaching the Adult Learner: Building Trust and Motivation. In J. Jones, M. Baran, & P. Cosgrove (Eds.), *Outcome-Based Strategies for Adult Learning* (pp. 12–33). Hershey, PA: IGI Global. doi:10.4018/978-1-5225-5712-8.ch002

Baron, A., & McNeal, K. (2019). Strategies for Teaching Online Higher Education Courses With an Eye Towards Retention: Choosing a Culturally Responsive Path. In L. Kyei-Blankson, J. Blankson, & E. Ntuli (Eds.), *Care and Culturally Responsive Pedagogy in Online Settings* (pp. 280–298). Hershey, PA: IGI Global. doi:10.4018/978-1-5225-7802-4.ch014

Bello-Bravo, J., & Lutomia, A. N. (2019). Changing Formal and Informal Learning Practices Using Smartphones: The Case of Market Women of Ghana. In D. Peltz & A. Clemons (Eds.), *Multicultural Andragogy for Transformative Learning* (pp. 171–193). Hershey, PA: IGI Global. doi:10.4018/978-1-5225-3474-7.ch010

Bishop, J. (2019). Supporting Millennials in Adult and Community Education Settings: Reflective Interviews With Caregivers in the Form of Parents and Guardians. In L. Kyei-Blankson, J. Blankson, & E. Ntuli (Eds.), *Care and Culturally Responsive Pedagogy in Online Settings* (pp. 299–330). Hershey, PA: IGI Global. doi:10.4018/978-1-5225-7802-4.ch015

Bradley, D. J. (2019). Effective Online Learning for Adults: Ragan's Principles Applied. In J. Jones, M. Baran, & P. Cosgrove (Eds.), *Outcome-Based Strategies for Adult Learning* (pp. 115–124). Hershey, PA: IGI Global. doi:10.4018/978-1-5225-5712-8.ch007

Brookfield, S. (2017). Teaching for Critical Thinking. In V. Wang (Ed.), *Adult Education and Vocational Training in the Digital Age* (pp. 1–17). Hershey, PA: IGI Global. doi:10.4018/978-1-5225-0929-5.ch001

Brookfield, S. (2017). The Essence of Powerful Teaching. In V. Wang (Ed.), *Adult Education and Vocational Training in the Digital Age* (pp. 184–199). Hershey, PA: IGI Global. doi:10.4018/978-1-5225-0929-5.ch011

Byrd, C., & Lansing, S. T. (2019). Putting Paint to Canvas: Artful Teaching Strategies for Teachers of Adult Learners. In J. Jones, M. Baran, & P. Cosgrove (Eds.), *Outcome-Based Strategies for Adult Learning* (pp. 56–83). Hershey, PA: IGI Global. doi:10.4018/978-1-5225-5712-8.ch004

Chai, M. T., Malik, A. S., Saad, M. N., & Rahman, M. A. (2019). Application of Digital Technologies, Multimedia, and Brain-Based Strategies: Nurturing Adult Education and Lifelong Learning. In J. Jones, M. Baran, & P. Cosgrove (Eds.), *Outcome-Based Strategies for Adult Learning* (pp. 148–179). Hershey, PA: IGI Global. doi:10.4018/978-1-5225-5712-8.ch009

Chang, B. (2017). Transformative Learning: Reader's Guide. *International Journal of Adult Vocational Education and Technology*, 8(1), 16–22. doi:10.4018/ijavet.2017010102

Charungkaittikul, S., & Henschke, J. A. (2017). Applying Andragogical Concepts in Creating a Sustainable Lifelong Learning Society. *International Journal of Adult Vocational Education and Technology*, 8(4), 38–51. doi:10.4018/IJAVET.2017100104

Cherrstrom, C. A., & Boden, C. J. (2018). Beacon of Hope: Award-Winning Program Redesign for Post-Traditional Students. *International Journal of Adult Vocational Education and Technology*, 9(2), 30–47. doi:10.4018/IJAVET.2018040103

Clemons, A. C. (2019). Manifesto for Critical Andragogy: A Liberating Critique to Adult Learning. In D. Peltz & A. Clemons (Eds.), *Multicultural Andragogy for Transformative Learning* (pp. 73–90). Hershey, PA: IGI Global. doi:10.4018/978-1-5225-3474-7.ch005

Cosgrove, P. B. (2019). The Nature of Success in Doctoral Education: The Roles of the Student, the Advisor, and Goals. In F. Giuseffi (Ed.), *Self-Directed Learning Strategies in Adult Educational Contexts* (pp. 90–109). Hershey, PA: IGI Global. doi:10.4018/978-1-5225-8018-8.ch005

Cypret-Mahach, R. (2018). Transformational Shifts of Pedagogy Through Professional Development, Essential Questions, and Self-Directed Learning. In F. Giuseffi (Ed.), *Emerging Self-Directed Learning Strategies in the Digital Age* (pp. 160–178). Hershey, PA: IGI Global. doi:10.4018/978-1-5225-3465-5.ch008

Derrick, M. G., & Wighting, M. (2019). Cultural Awareness Research and Implications for Practice and Professional Development. In D. Peltz & A. Clemons (Eds.), *Multicultural Andragogy for Transformative Learning* (pp. 1–8). Hershey, PA: IGI Global. doi:10.4018/978-1-5225-3474-7.ch001

Dietlin, O. R., Loomis, J. S., & Preffer, J. (2019). Pedagogy of Authenticity in the Online Learning Environment: An Interdisciplinary Overview. In L. Kyei-Blankson, J. Blankson, & E. Ntuli (Eds.), *Care and Culturally Responsive Pedagogy in Online Settings* (pp. 214–229). Hershey, PA: IGI Global. doi:10.4018/978-1-5225-7802-4.ch011

Dimmitt, E. J. (2019). Arts Integration Techniques in the Adult Learning Environment. In J. Jones, M. Baran, & P. Cosgrove (Eds.), *Outcome-Based Strategies for Adult Learning* (pp. 34–55). Hershey, PA: IGI Global. doi:10.4018/978-1-5225-5712-8.ch003

Dimmitt, E. J. (2019). Professional Learning Communities and Adult Learning and Teaching: Best Practices in Building a Community of Learners. In J. Jones, M. Baran, & P. Cosgrove (Eds.), *Outcome-Based Strategies for Adult Learning* (pp. 125–147). Hershey, PA: IGI Global. doi:10.4018/978-1-5225-5712-8.ch008

Doulik, P., Skoda, J., & Simonova, I. (2017). Learning Styles in the e-Learning Environment: The Approaches and Research on Longitudinal Changes. *International Journal of Distance Education Technologies, 15*(2), 45–61. doi:10.4018/IJDET.2017040104

Drago-Severson, E., Maslin-Ostrowski, P., & Hoffman, A. M. (2017). In One Voice: Aspiring and Practicing School Leaders Embrace the Need for a More Integrated Approach to Leadership Preparation and Development. In V. Wang (Ed.), *Adult Education and Vocational Training in the Digital Age* (pp. 147–168). Hershey, PA: IGI Global. doi:10.4018/978-1-5225-0929-5.ch009

Duthely, L. M., Nunn, S. G., & Avella, J. T. (2019). Spirituality and Religion as Cultural Influences in Andragogy. In D. Peltz & A. Clemons (Eds.), *Multicultural Andragogy for Transformative Learning* (pp. 45–72). Hershey, PA: IGI Global. doi:10.4018/978-1-5225-3474-7.ch004

Elmahjoub, A., & Lamb, T. (2019). Learner Autonomy: A Cultural Perspective From Libya. In F. Giuseffi (Ed.), *Self-Directed Learning Strategies in Adult Educational Contexts* (pp. 71–89). Hershey, PA: IGI Global. doi:10.4018/978-1-5225-8018-8.ch004

Falcade, A., Krassmann, A. L., Medina, R. D., & Freitas, V. C. (2019). Instructional Design Applied to TCN5 Virtual World. In Y. Vovides & L. Lemus (Eds.), *Optimizing Instructional Design Methods in Higher Education* (pp. 147–175). Hershey, PA: IGI Global. doi:10.4018/978-1-5225-4975-8.ch008

Fallahi, M. (2019). Assessment of Learning in Higher Education. In J. Jones, M. Baran, & P. Cosgrove (Eds.), *Outcome-Based Strategies for Adult Learning* (pp. 196–217). Hershey, PA: IGI Global. doi:10.4018/978-1-5225-5712-8.ch011

Fallahi, M. (2019). Making Instruction Work for Adult Learners. In J. Jones, M. Baran, & P. Cosgrove (Eds.), *Outcome-Based Strategies for Adult Learning* (pp. 1–11). Hershey, PA: IGI Global. doi:10.4018/978-1-5225-5712-8.ch001

Farmer, L. S. (2019). Globalization and Localization in Online Settings. In L. Kyei-Blankson, J. Blankson, & E. Ntuli (Eds.), *Care and Culturally Responsive Pedagogy in Online Settings* (pp. 168–191). Hershey, PA: IGI Global. doi:10.4018/978-1-5225-7802-4.ch009

Farrelly, W., & Linse, C. (2019). Learning How to Clarify Complex Concepts for Children Through Naturalistic Inquiry: Moving Beyond Simplification. In F. Giuseffi (Ed.), *Self-Directed Learning Strategies in Adult Educational Contexts* (pp. 183–205). Hershey, PA: IGI Global. doi:10.4018/978-1-5225-8018-8.ch009

Fleming, T. (2018). Critical Theory and Transformative Learning: Rethinking the Radical Intent of Mezirow's Theory. *International Journal of Adult Vocational Education and Technology*, 9(3), 1–13. doi:10.4018/IJAVET.2018070101

Fletcher, E. C. Jr, Lasonen, J. L., & Hernandez-Gantes, V. M. (2017). What Is CTE?: Practitioners Struggle to Define Their Field in the United States. In V. Wang (Ed.), *Adult Education and Vocational Training in the Digital Age* (pp. 241–257). Hershey, PA: IGI Global. doi:10.4018/978-1-5225-0929-5.ch014

Gaimaro, A., & Lomellini, A. (2019). Designing Innovative Faculty Development Initiatives Through the Lens of the Adult Learner. In F. Giuseffi (Ed.), *Self-Directed Learning Strategies in Adult Educational Contexts* (pp. 206–230). Hershey, PA: IGI Global. doi:10.4018/978-1-5225-8018-8.ch010

Gibson, P. (2017). The Need for Imagination and Creativity in Instructional Design. In V. Wang (Ed.), *Adult Education and Vocational Training in the Digital Age* (pp. 134–146). Hershey, PA: IGI Global. doi:10.4018/978-1-5225-0929-5.ch008

Giering, J. A., & Hunger, G. M. (2019). Advancing a New General Education Curriculum Through a Faculty Community of Practice: A Model for Intentional Design. In Y. Vovides & L. Lemus (Eds.), *Optimizing Instructional Design Methods in Higher Education* (pp. 27–47). Hershey, PA: IGI Global. doi:10.4018/978-1-5225-4975-8.ch003

Giuseffi, F. G. (2019). The Socratic Way and Adult Learning: Exploring a Nelsonian View of the Socratic Method in Self-Directed Learning Encounters. In F. Giuseffi (Ed.), *Self-Directed Learning Strategies in Adult Educational Contexts* (pp. 110–123). Hershey, PA: IGI Global. doi:10.4018/978-1-5225-8018-8.ch006

Gotian, R. (2019). Integrating Cultural Perspectives Into Organizational Learning: An Anecdotal Study in Higher Education. In D. Peltz & A. Clemons (Eds.), *Multicultural Andragogy for Transformative Learning* (pp. 224–240). Hershey, PA: IGI Global. doi:10.4018/978-1-5225-3474-7.ch013

Grant, P. L. (2019). Undergraduate Student Perception of Caring and Trust: How Those May Relate to Student Engagement in Self-Directed Learning. In F. Giuseffi (Ed.), *Self-Directed Learning Strategies in Adult Educational Contexts* (pp. 23–43). Hershey, PA: IGI Global. doi:10.4018/978-1-5225-8018-8.ch002

Green, K. R., & Tolman, S. (2019). Equitable Means Accessible: Using Universal Design for Learning and Student Development Theory to Inform Online Pedagogy. In L. Kyei-Blankson, J. Blankson, & E. Ntuli (Eds.), *Care and Culturally Responsive Pedagogy in Online Settings* (pp. 125–147). Hershey, PA: IGI Global. doi:10.4018/978-1-5225-7802-4.ch007

Heitner, K. L., Sherman, K. C., & Jennings, M. E. (2019). Care and Cultural Responsiveness of Online College Courses: Preliminary Criteria and Best Practices. In L. Kyei-Blankson, J. Blankson, & E. Ntuli (Eds.), *Care and Culturally Responsive Pedagogy in Online Settings* (pp. 331–355). Hershey, PA: IGI Global. doi:10.4018/978-1-5225-7802-4.ch016

Holmgren, R. (2017). Digital Technologies as a Change Agent in Problem-Based Activities: A Comparison of Online and Campus-Based PBL in Swedish Firefighter Training. In V. Wang (Ed.), *Adult Education and Vocational Training in the Digital Age* (pp. 58–74). Hershey, PA: IGI Global. doi:10.4018/978-1-5225-0929-5.ch004

James, A., & Brookfield, S. (2017). The Serious Use of Play and Metaphor: LEGO® Models and Labyrinths. In V. Wang (Ed.), *Adult Education and Vocational Training in the Digital Age* (pp. 118–133). Hershey, PA: IGI Global. doi:10.4018/978-1-5225-0929-5.ch007

Jonas, P. M. (2019). Theories and Practice of Humor for Adult Instruction. In J. Jones, M. Baran, & P. Cosgrove (Eds.), *Outcome-Based Strategies for Adult Learning* (pp. 93–114). Hershey, PA: IGI Global. doi:10.4018/978-1-5225-5712-8.ch006

Jones, J. E., Baran, M. L., & Steuber, J. A. (2019). Effective Teaching Strategies to Connect With the Adult Learners' Worldview. In J. Jones, M. Baran, & P. Cosgrove (Eds.), *Outcome-Based Strategies for Adult Learning* (pp. 84–92). Hershey, PA: IGI Global. doi:10.4018/978-1-5225-5712-8.ch005

Kan, Q., & Tang, J. (2018). Researching Mobile-Assisted English Language Learning Among Adult Distance Learners in China: Emerging Practices and Learner Perception of Teacher Role. *International Journal of Computer-Assisted Language Learning and Teaching*, 8(3), 1–28. doi:10.4018/IJCALLT.2018070101

Khan, M. S., Nambobi, M., & Ali, M. S. (2018). MOOCs in TVET Sectors of Developing Countries: Benefits, Possibilities, and Challenges. In F. Giuseffi (Ed.), *Emerging Self-Directed Learning Strategies in the Digital Age* (pp. 22–47). Hershey, PA: IGI Global. doi:10.4018/978-1-5225-3465-5.ch003

Kilburn, M., Radu, M. B., & Henckell, M. (2019). Conceptual and Theoretical Frameworks for CRT Pedagogy. In L. Kyei-Blankson, J. Blankson, & E. Ntuli (Eds.), *Care and Culturally Responsive Pedagogy in Online Settings* (pp. 1–21). Hershey, PA: IGI Global. doi:10.4018/978-1-5225-7802-4.ch001

Kızıl, A. Ş. (2019). Computer-Assisted Language Learning and Design for Learning: Potential Synergies. In Y. Vovides & L. Lemus (Eds.), *Optimizing Instructional Design Methods in Higher Education* (pp. 129–146). Hershey, PA: IGI Global. doi:10.4018/978-1-5225-4975-8.ch007

Kumi-Yeboah, A., Dogbey, J., Yuan, G., & Amponsah, S. (2019). Cultural Diversity in Online Learning: Perceptions of Minority Graduate Students. In L. Kyei-Blankson, J. Blankson, & E. Ntuli (Eds.), *Care and Culturally Responsive Pedagogy in Online Settings* (pp. 230–251). Hershey, PA: IGI Global. doi:10.4018/978-1-5225-7802-4.ch012

Lemus, L. R., & Vovides, Y. (2019). The Role of Instructional Design in Surfacing the Hidden Curriculum. In Y. Vovides & L. Lemus (Eds.), *Optimizing Instructional Design Methods in Higher Education* (pp. 176–182). Hershey, PA: IGI Global. doi:10.4018/978-1-5225-4975-8.ch009

Lim, D. H., You, J., Kim, J., & Hwang, J. (2019). Instructional Design for Adult and Continuing Higher Education: Theoretical and Practical Considerations. In Y. Vovides & L. Lemus (Eds.), *Optimizing Instructional Design Methods in Higher Education* (pp. 73–100). Hershey, PA: IGI Global. doi:10.4018/978-1-5225-4975-8.ch005

Long, J. D. (2018). The Intersection of Andragogy and Dissertation Writing: How Andragogy Can Improve the Process. In F. Giuseffi (Ed.), *Emerging Self-Directed Learning Strategies in the Digital Age* (pp. 81-108). Hershey, PA: IGI Global. doi:10.4018/978-1-5225-3465-5.ch005

Lutomia, A. N., & Wanzala, W. O. (2019). Intersecting Gender and Culture: Indigenous Andragogical Practices in Western Kenya. In D. Peltz & A. Clemons (Eds.), *Multicultural Andragogy for Transformative Learning* (pp. 154–170). Hershey, PA: IGI Global. doi:10.4018/978-1-5225-3474-7.ch009

Mariano, G. J., & Batchelor, K. (2018). The Role of Metacogntion and Knowledge Transfer in Self-Directed Learning. In F. Giuseffi (Ed.), *Emerging Self-Directed Learning Strategies in the Digital Age* (pp. 141–159). Hershey, PA: IGI Global. doi:10.4018/978-1-5225-3465-5.ch007

Marzano, G., & Siguencia, L. O. (2019). Online Participatory Learning for Low-Qualified Adult Learners. *International Journal of Web-Based Learning and Teaching Technologies, 14*(2), 50–66. doi:10.4018/IJWLTT.2019040104

Mattera, M., & Chassonnaud, L. F. (2019). Mixing Cultures Through Intercultural Methodology (MTM): A Qualitative Study of Andragogical Approaches. In D. Peltz & A. Clemons (Eds.), *Multicultural Andragogy for Transformative Learning* (pp. 133–153). Hershey, PA: IGI Global. doi:10.4018/978-1-5225-3474-7.ch008

Miles, D. A. (2019). Autonomous Learning as a Transformative Experience. In D. Peltz & A. Clemons (Eds.), *Multicultural Andragogy for Transformative Learning* (pp. 9–29). Hershey, PA: IGI Global. doi:10.4018/978-1-5225-3474-7.ch002

Montelongo, R., & Eaton, P. W. (2019). Strategies and Reflections on Teaching Diversity in Digital Learning Space(s). In L. Kyei-Blankson, J. Blankson, & E. Ntuli (Eds.), *Care and Culturally Responsive Pedagogy in Online Settings* (pp. 41–62). Hershey, PA: IGI Global. doi:10.4018/978-1-5225-7802-4.ch003

Mthembu, N. (2019). Ushering Transformative Change: Infusing De-Colonized Cultural Changes Into South African Curriculum and Andragogical Practices. In D. Peltz & A. Clemons (Eds.), *Multicultural Andragogy for Transformative Learning* (pp. 194–206). Hershey, PA: IGI Global. doi:10.4018/978-1-5225-3474-7.ch011

Neimann, T., & Wang, V. X. (2017). Deep Learning and Online Education as an Informal Learning Process: Is There a Relationship between Deep Learning and Online Education as an Informal Learning Process? In V. Wang (Ed.), *Adult Education and Vocational Training in the Digital Age* (pp. 37–57). Hershey, PA: IGI Global. doi:10.4018/978-1-5225-0929-5.ch003

Nerstrom, N. (2017). Transformative Learning: Moving Beyond Theory and Practice. *International Journal of Adult Vocational Education and Technology*, *8*(1), 36–46. doi:10.4018/ijavet.2017010104

Nussli, N., Guan, Y., & Oh, K. (2019). Strategies to Support Teachers in Designing Culturally Responsive Curricula in Online Learning Environments. In L. Kyei-Blankson, J. Blankson, & E. Ntuli (Eds.), *Care and Culturally Responsive Pedagogy in Online Settings* (pp. 252–279). Hershey, PA: IGI Global. doi:10.4018/978-1-5225-7802-4.ch013

Orlando, M., & Howard, L. (2018). Setting the Stage for Success in an Online Learning Environment. In F. Giuseffi (Ed.), *Emerging Self-Directed Learning Strategies in the Digital Age* (pp. 1–9). Hershey, PA: IGI Global. doi:10.4018/978-1-5225-3465-5.ch001

Park, S., Lim, D. H., & Kim, M. (2019). Instructional Design in Human Resource Development Academic Programs in the USA. In Y. Vovides & L. Lemus (Eds.), *Optimizing Instructional Design Methods in Higher Education* (pp. 48–72). Hershey, PA: IGI Global. doi:10.4018/978-1-5225-4975-8.ch004

Peltz, D. P. (2019). Andragogy, Culture, and Adult Learning Worldviews. In D. Peltz & A. Clemons (Eds.), *Multicultural Andragogy for Transformative Learning* (pp. 92–114). Hershey, PA: IGI Global. doi:10.4018/978-1-5225-3474-7.ch006

Perez, A. (2019). Cultural Considerations in Postsecondary and Vocational Education: A Discussion on Equity and Accessibility. In D. Peltz & A. Clemons (Eds.), *Multicultural Andragogy for Transformative Learning* (pp. 208–223). Hershey, PA: IGI Global. doi:10.4018/978-1-5225-3474-7.ch012

Pillay, H., Watters, J. J., Flynn, M. C., & Hoff, L. (2017). Public-Private Partnership Principles Applied to Industry-School Partnership to Support Technical and Vocational Education. In V. Wang (Ed.), *Adult Education and Vocational Training in the Digital Age* (pp. 18–36). Hershey, PA: IGI Global. doi:10.4018/978-1-5225-0929-5.ch002

Re'vell, M. (2019). Toward Culturally Restorative: Teaching Approaches. In L. Kyei-Blankson, J. Blankson, & E. Ntuli (Eds.), *Care and Culturally Responsive Pedagogy in Online Settings* (pp. 148–167). Hershey, PA: IGI Global. doi:10.4018/978-1-5225-7802-4.ch008

Reio, T. G. Jr, & Trudel, J. (2017). Workplace Incivility and Conflict Management Styles: Predicting Job Performance, Organizational Commitment, and Turnover Intent. In V. Wang (Ed.), *Adult Education and Vocational Training in the Digital Age* (pp. 217–240). Hershey, PA: IGI Global. doi:10.4018/978-1-5225-0929-5.ch013

Rhodes, C. M. (2018). Culturally Responsive Teaching with Adult Learners: A Review of the Literature. *International Journal of Adult Vocational Education and Technology*, 9(4), 33–41. doi:10.4018/IJAVET.2018100103

Rhodes, C. M., & Lohr, K. D. (2019). Culturally Inclusive Teaching of Adult English Language Learners. In D. Peltz & A. Clemons (Eds.), *Multicultural Andragogy for Transformative Learning* (pp. 115–132). Hershey, PA: IGI Global. doi:10.4018/978-1-5225-3474-7.ch007

Rice, R. O. (2019). Analyzing How Cultural Norms Affect Learner Preferences in Organizational Learning Programs. In D. Peltz & A. Clemons (Eds.), *Multicultural Andragogy for Transformative Learning* (pp. 241–251). Hershey, PA: IGI Global. doi:10.4018/978-1-5225-3474-7.ch014

Rider, J. (2019). E-Relationships: Using Computer-Mediated Discourse Analysis to Build Ethics of Care in Digital Spaces. In L. Kyei-Blankson, J. Blankson, & E. Ntuli (Eds.), *Care and Culturally Responsive Pedagogy in Online Settings* (pp. 192–212). Hershey, PA: IGI Global. doi:10.4018/978-1-5225-7802-4.ch010

Russell, F. R. (2019). Adult Learners: Standards for Teacher Effectiveness and Conditions for Optimal Learning. In J. Jones, M. Baran, & P. Cosgrove (Eds.), *Outcome-Based Strategies for Adult Learning* (pp. 180–195). Hershey, PA: IGI Global. doi:10.4018/978-1-5225-5712-8.ch010

Şentürk, C., & Zeybek, G. (2019). Overview of Learning From Past to Present and Self-Directed Learning. In F. Giuseffi (Ed.), *Self-Directed Learning Strategies in Adult Educational Contexts* (pp. 138–182). Hershey, PA: IGI Global. doi:10.4018/978-1-5225-8018-8.ch008

Setlhodi, I. I. (2019). The Value of Pacing in Promoting Self-Directed Learning. In F. Giuseffi (Ed.), *Self-Directed Learning Strategies in Adult Educational Contexts* (pp. 1–22). Hershey, PA: IGI Global. doi:10.4018/978-1-5225-8018-8.ch001

Shi, H., & Witte, M. M. (2018). Self-Directed Language Learning, Asian Cultural Influences, and the Teacher's Role. In F. Giuseffi (Ed.), *Emerging Self-Directed Learning Strategies in the Digital Age* (pp. 109–140). Hershey, PA: IGI Global. doi:10.4018/978-1-5225-3465-5.ch006

Shishigu, A., Michael, K., & Atnafu, M. (2019). Can Blended Learning Enhance Students' Tendency to Regulate Their Own Learning?: An Experience From Pedagogical Experiments. In F. Giuseffi (Ed.), *Self-Directed Learning Strategies in Adult Educational Contexts* (pp. 44–70). Hershey, PA: IGI Global. doi:10.4018/978-1-5225-8018-8.ch003

Starr-Glass, D. (2019). Culturally Responsive Pedagogy, National Culture, and Online Instruction: Leading to Learning. In L. Kyei-Blankson, J. Blankson, & E. Ntuli (Eds.), *Care and Culturally Responsive Pedagogy in Online Settings* (pp. 89–108). Hershey, PA: IGI Global. doi:10.4018/978-1-5225-7802-4.ch005

Stevenson, C. N. (2019). Creating Connections: Competency-Based Degree Programs and Undergraduate Capstone Courses for Adult Learners. In J. Jones, M. Baran, & P. Cosgrove (Eds.), *Outcome-Based Strategies for Adult Learning* (pp. 218–240). Hershey, PA: IGI Global. doi:10.4018/978-1-5225-5712-8.ch012

Sutha, J. (2018). Exploring the Role of Adult Learning Theory in Understanding Employees' Participation in Non-Mandatory Training. In F. Giuseffi (Ed.), *Emerging Self-Directed Learning Strategies in the Digital Age* (pp. 48–80). Hershey, PA: IGI Global. doi:10.4018/978-1-5225-3465-5.ch004

Taylor, M., Vaughan, N., Ghani, S. K., Atas, S., & Fairbrother, M. (2018). Looking Back and Looking Forward: A Glimpse of Blended Learning in Higher Education From 2007-2017. *International Journal of Adult Vocational Education and Technology*, 9(1), 1–14. doi:10.4018/IJAVET.2018010101

Taylor, M. C., Atas, S., & Ghani, S. (2019). Alternate Dimensions of Cognitive Presence for Blended Learning in Higher Education. *International Journal of Mobile and Blended Learning, 11*(2), 1–18. doi:10.4018/IJMBL.2019040101

Umar, M. A., Shuru, A., Kufena, A. M., Tanko, M. Y., Sambo, A. A., & Hassan, S. A. (2018). Mobile CGPA Monitoring System: A Tool to Guide Self-Directed Learning. In F. Giuseffi (Ed.), *Emerging Self-Directed Learning Strategies in the Digital Age* (pp. 10–21). Hershey, PA: IGI Global. doi:10.4018/978-1-5225-3465-5.ch002

Vovides, Y., & Lemus, L. R. (2019). The Evolving Landscape of Instructional Design in Higher Education. In Y. Vovides & L. Lemus (Eds.), *Optimizing Instructional Design Methods in Higher Education* (pp. 1–8). Hershey, PA: IGI Global. doi:10.4018/978-1-5225-4975-8.ch001

Wang, C., Chen, X., Edgar, D., & Zhao, Y. (2017). The Demand, Content, and Entrance Criteria of Operations Management Programmes under the Context of Internationalization: An Empirical Comparative Investigation. In V. Wang (Ed.), *Adult Education and Vocational Training in the Digital Age* (pp. 75–97). Hershey, PA: IGI Global. doi:10.4018/978-1-5225-0929-5.ch005

Wang, V. X., & Neimann, T. (2017). Internet Technologies and Online Learning. In V. Wang (Ed.), *Adult Education and Vocational Training in the Digital Age* (pp. 98–117). Hershey, PA: IGI Global. doi:10.4018/978-1-5225-0929-5.ch006

Williams, Y. (2019). Culturally Responsive Teaching and Inclusion for Online Students With Exceptionalities and Other Needs. In L. Kyei-Blankson, J. Blankson, & E. Ntuli (Eds.), *Care and Culturally Responsive Pedagogy in Online Settings* (pp. 109–124). Hershey, PA: IGI Global. doi:10.4018/978-1-5225-7802-4.ch006

Willis, P. (2017). Learning Physical and Digital Conviviality through Practice Stories. In V. Wang (Ed.), *Adult Education and Vocational Training in the Digital Age* (pp. 169–183). Hershey, PA: IGI Global. doi:10.4018/978-1-5225-0929-5.ch010

Wilson, J. H. (2019). Andragogy and the Learning-Tech Culture Revolution: The Internet of Things (IoT), Blockchain, AI, and the Disruption of Learning. In D. Peltz & A. Clemons (Eds.), *Multicultural Andragogy for Transformative Learning* (pp. 252–269). Hershey, PA: IGI Global. doi:10.4018/978-1-5225-3474-7.ch015

Related Readings

Zimmerman, A. S., & Kim, J. (2017). Excavating and (Re)presenting Stories: Narrative Inquiry as an Emergent Methodology in the Field of Adult Vocational Education and Technology. *International Journal of Adult Vocational Education and Technology, 8*(2), 16–28. doi:10.4018/IJAVET.2017040102

About the Contributors

Lorie Cook-Benjamin has worked in higher education for over 30 years. Her areas of expertise include curriculum, assessment, pedagogical practices, instructional strategies, and student engagement in both online and face-to-face teaching environments. She is a reviewer for and published author in various peer-reviewed journals. As a tenured faculty member and higher education administrator, her work experiences offer a unique lens to assist in navigating needed higher education changes to meet the learning expectations of today's students.

Jared Cook graduated in 2016 with an M.S.E. in Higher Education Student Affairs at Fort Hays State University in Hays, KS. Presently, he is finishing his final class and is set to graduate in August 2019 with an Ed.D. in Educational Administration and Leadership, with an emphasis in Adult and Higher Education. He currently works for the University of South Dakota as a graduate research assistant, as well as teaches for Upward Bound.

Index

Purchase Print, E-Book, or Print + E-Book

IGI Global's reference books can now be purchased from three unique pricing formats:
Print Only, E-Book Only, or Print + E-Book.
Shipping fees may apply.
www.igi-global.com

Recommended Reference Books

ISBN: 978-1-5225-9348-5
© 2019; 454 pp.
List Price: $255

ISBN: 978-1-5225-7763-8
© 2019; 253 pp.
List Price: $175

ISBN: 978-1-5225-7531-3
© 2019; 324 pp.
List Price: $185

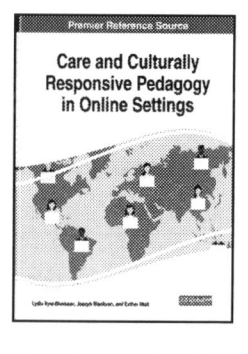

ISBN: 978-1-5225-7802-4
© 2019; 423 pp.
List Price: $195

ISBN: 978-1-5225-6246-7
© 2019; 610 pp.
List Price: $275

ISBN: 978-1-5225-2998-9
© 2018; 352 pp.
List Price: $195

Looking for free content, product updates, news, and special offers?
Join IGI Global's mailing list today and start enjoying exclusive perks sent only to IGI Global members.
Add your name to the list at **www.igi-global.com/newsletters**.

Publisher of Peer-Reviewed, Timely, and Innovative Academic Research

IGI Global
DISSEMINATOR OF KNOWLEDGE

www.igi-global.com · Sign up at www.igi-global.com/newsletters · facebook.com/igiglobal · twitter.com/igiglobal

Ensure Quality Research is Introduced to the Academic Community

Become an IGI Global Reviewer for Authored Book Projects

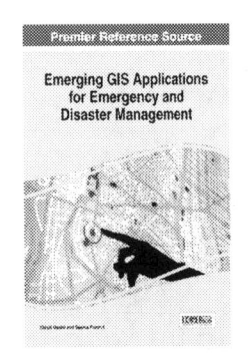
Emerging GIS Applications for Emergency and Disaster Management

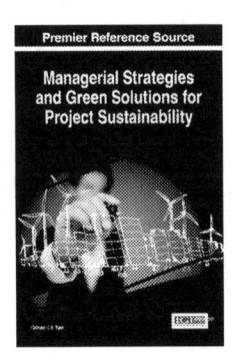
Managerial Strategies and Green Solutions for Project Sustainability

Comparative Approaches to Using R and Python for Statistical Data Analysis

Solutions for High-Touch Communications in a High-Tech World

The overall success of an authored book project is dependent on quality and timely reviews.

In this competitive age of scholarly publishing, constructive and timely feedback significantly expedites the turnaround time of manuscripts from submission to acceptance, allowing the publication and discovery of forward-thinking research at a much more expeditious rate. Several IGI Global authored book projects are currently seeking highly-qualified experts in the field to fill vacancies on their respective editorial review boards:

Applications and Inquiries may be sent to:
development@igi-global.com

Applicants must have a doctorate (or an equivalent degree) as well as publishing and reviewing experience. Reviewers are asked to complete the open-ended evaluation questions with as much detail as possible in a timely, collegial, and constructive manner. All reviewers' tenures run for one-year terms on the editorial review boards and are expected to complete at least three reviews per term. Upon successful completion of this term, reviewers can be considered for an additional term.

If you have a colleague that may be interested in this opportunity, we encourage you to share this information with them.

www.igi-global.com

IGI Global Proudly Partners with

eContent Pro International® Publication Services
Committed to Excellent Service, Affordability, and the Highest Quality
From Manuscript Development to Publication

Publication Services Provided by eContent Pro International:

Scientific & Scholarly Editing

English Language Copy Editing

Journal Recommendation

Typesetting & Publishing

Figure, Table, Chart & Equation Conversions

Translation

**IGI Global Authors Save 25% on
eContent Pro International's Services!**

Scan the QR Code to Receive Your 25% Discount

The 25% discount is applied directly to your eContent Pro International shopping cart when placing an order through IGI Global's referral link. Use the QR code to access this referral link. eContent Pro International has the right to end or modify any promotion at any time.

Email: customerservice@econtentpro.com   **econtentpro.com**

 **IGI Global**
DISSEMINATOR OF KNOWLEDGE
www.igi-global.com

Celebrating Over 30 Years of Scholarly
Knowledge Creation & Dissemination

 **InfoSci®-Books**

A Database of Over 5,300+ Reference Books Containing Over
100,000+ Chapters Focusing on Emerging Research

GAIN ACCESS TO **THOUSANDS** OF
REFERENCE BOOKS AT **A FRACTION**
OF THEIR INDIVIDUAL LIST **PRICE**.

InfoSci®-Books Database

The **InfoSci®-Books** database is a collection of
over 5,300+ IGI Global single and multi-volume
reference books, handbooks of research, and
encyclopedias, encompassing groundbreaking
research from prominent experts worldwide that
span over 350+ topics in 11 core subject areas
including business, computer science, education,
science and engineering, social sciences and more.

Open Access Fee Waiver (Offset Model) Initiative

For any library that invests in IGI Global's InfoSci-Journals and/
or InfoSci-Books databases, IGI Global will match the library's
investment with a fund of equal value to go toward **subsidizing
the OA article processing charges (APCs) for their students,
faculty, and staff** at that institution when their work is submitted
and accepted under OA into an IGI Global journal.*

INFOSCI® PLATFORM FEATURES

- No DRM
- No Set-Up or Maintenance Fees
- A Guarantee of No More Than a
  5% Annual Increase
- Full-Text HTML and PDF
  Viewing Options
- Downloadable MARC Records
- Unlimited Simultaneous Access
- COUNTER 5 Compliant Reports
- Formatted Citations With Ability to
  Export to RefWorks and EasyBib
- No Embargo of Content (Research
  is Available Months in Advance of
  the Print Release)

*The fund will be offered on an annual basis and expire at the end of
the subscription period. The fund would renew as the subscription is
renewed for each year thereafter. The open access fees will be waived
after the student, faculty, or staff's paper has been vetted and accepted
into an IGI Global journal and the fund can only be used toward
publishing OA in an IGI Global journal. Libraries in developing countries
will have the match on their investment doubled.

To Learn More or To Purchase This Database:
www.igi-global.com/infosci-books

eresources@igi-global.com • Toll Free: 1-866-342-6657 ext. 100 • Phone: 717-533-8845 x100

 **IGI Global**
DISSEMINATOR OF KNOWLEDGE

www.igi-global.com

www.igi-global.com

Publisher of Peer-Reviewed, Timely, and
Innovative Academic Research Since 1988

IGI Global's Transformative Open Access (OA) Model:
How to Turn Your University Library's Database Acquisitions Into a Source of OA Funding

In response to the OA movement and well in advance of Plan S, IGI Global, early last year, unveiled their OA Fee Waiver (Offset Model) Initiative.

Under this initiative, librarians who invest in IGI Global's InfoSci-Books (5,300+ reference books) and/or InfoSci-Journals (185+ scholarly journals) databases will be able to subsidize their patron's OA article processing charges (APC) when their work is submitted and accepted (after the peer review process) into an IGI Global journal.*

How Does it Work?

1. When a library subscribes or perpetually purchases IGI Global's InfoSci-Databases including InfoSci-Books (5,300+ e-books), InfoSci-Journals (185+ e-journals), and/or their discipline/subject-focused subsets, IGI Global will match the library's investment with a fund of equal value to go toward subsidizing the OA article processing charges (APCs) for their patrons.

   Researchers: Be sure to recommend the InfoSci-Books and InfoSci-Journals to take advantage of this initiative.

2. When a student, faculty, or staff member submits a paper and it is accepted (following the peer review) into one of IGI Global's 185+ scholarly journals, the author will have the option to have their paper published under a traditional publishing model or as OA.

3. When the author chooses to have their paper published under OA, IGI Global will notify them of the OA Fee Waiver (Offset Model) Initiative. If the author decides they would like to take advantage of this initiative, IGI Global will deduct the US$ 1,500 APC from the created fund.

4. This fund will be offered on an annual basis and will renew as the subscription is renewed for each year thereafter. IGI Global will manage the fund and award the APC waivers unless the librarian has a preference as to how the funds should be managed.

Hear From the Experts on This Initiative:

"I'm very happy to have been able to make one of my recent research contributions, 'Visualizing the Social Media Conversations of a National Information Technology Professional Association' featured in the *International Journal of Human Capital and Information Technology Professionals*, freely available along with having access to the valuable resources found within IGI Global's InfoSci-Journals database."

– **Prof. Stuart Palmer**,
Deakin University, Australia

For More Information, Visit: www.igi-global.com/publish/contributor-resources/open-access or contact IGI Global's Database Team at eresources@igi-global.com

ARE YOU READY TO PUBLISH YOUR RESEARCH?

IGI Global
DISSEMINATOR OF KNOWLEDGE

IGI Global offers book authorship and editorship opportunities across 11 subject areas, including business, computer science, education, science and engineering, social sciences, and more!

Benefits of Publishing with IGI Global:

- Free, one-on-one editorial and promotional support.
- Expedited publishing timelines that can take your book from start to finish in less than one (1) year.
- Choose from a variety of formats including: Edited and Authored References, Handbooks of Research, Encyclopedias, and Research Insights.
- Utilize IGI Global's eEditorial Discovery® submission system in support of conducting the submission and blind review process.

- IGI Global maintains a strict adherence to ethical practices due in part to our full membership with the Committee on Publication Ethics (COPE).
- Indexing potential in prestigious indices such as Scopus®, Web of Science™, PsycINFO®, and ERIC – Education Resources Information Center.
- Ability to connect your ORCID iD to your IGI Global publications.
- Earn royalties on your publication as well as receive complimentary copies and exclusive discounts.

Get Started Today by Contacting the Acquisitions Department at:
acquisition@igi-global.com

www.igi-global.com/infosci-ondemand

InfoSci®-OnDemand

Continuously updated with new material on a weekly basis, InfoSci®-OnDemand offers the ability to search through thousands of quality full-text research papers. Users can narrow each search by identifying key topic areas of interest, then display a complete listing of relevant papers, and purchase materials specific to their research needs.

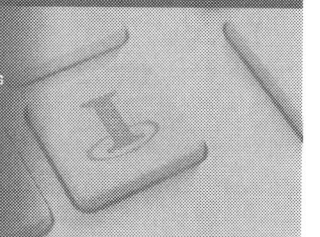

Comprehensive Service

- Over 125,000+ journal articles, book chapters, and case studies.
- All content is downloadable in PDF and HTML format and can be stored locally for future use.

No Subscription Fees

- One time fee of $37.50 per PDF download.

Instant Access

- Receive a download link immediately after order completion!

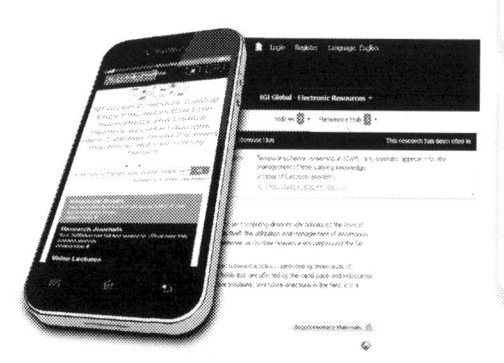

"It really provides an excellent entry into the research literature of the field. It presents a manageable number of highly relevant sources on topics of interest to a wide range of researchers. The sources are scholarly, but also accessible to 'practitioners'."

- Lisa Stimatz, MLS, University of North Carolina at Chapel Hill, USA

"It is an excellent and well designed database which will facilitate research, publication, and teaching. It is a very useful tool to have."

- George Ditsa, PhD, University of Wollongong, Australia

"I have accessed the database and find it to be a valuable tool to the IT/IS community. I found valuable articles meeting my search criteria 95% of the time."

- Prof. Lynda Louis, Xavier University of Louisiana, USA

Recommended for use by researchers who wish to immediately download PDFs of individual chapters or articles.

www.igi-global.com/e-resources/infosci-ondemand

IGI Global
DISSEMINATOR OF KNOWLEDGE

www.igi-global.com